Pangaea.
Why it tastes
so good.

Pangaea.
Why it tastes
so good.

By Martin Kouprie
Photography by James Tse

KEY PORTER BOOKS

Library and Archives Canada Cataloguing in Publication

Kouprie, Martin
            Pangaea / Martin Kouprie.

ISBN 978-1-55470-263-3

            1. Cookery. 2. Pangaea (Restaurant). I. Title.

TX715.6.K69 2010   641.509713'541   C2010-901889-3

ONTARIO ARTS COUNCIL
CONSEIL DES ARTS DE L'ONTARIO

The publisher gratefully acknowledges the support of the Canada Council for the Arts and the Ontario Arts Council for its publishing program. We acknowledge the support of the Government of Ontario through the Ontario Media Development Corporation's Ontario Book Initiative.

We acknowledge the financial support of the Government of Canada through the Canada Book Fund (CBF) for our publishing activities.

Key Porter Books
34 Nixon Road
Bolton, Ontario
Canada L7E 1W2

www.keyporter.com

Design: John Speakman
Printed and bound in Canada

MIX
Paper from
responsible sources
FSC™ C016245

10 11 12 13 14 6 5 4 3 2 1

I first became interested in cooking when I was a boy of 12 or so; I started reading my mother's *Gourmet* magazines and on those pages I saw inspiring recipes and learned that men could cook, too (in our house my mother ruled the stove). Reading about the dynamic, interesting men and women in the food industry opened my eyes to a new world and that world made a lasting impression on me.

So, in thanks I dedicate this book to the memory of *Gourmet* magazine, without which I'd likely be in another profession entirely.

pangaea

Contents

Contents

About Using This Book

All the recipes in this book are written assuming that you will use clean, dry, best-quality produce of average size. If a larger or smaller item is required, we've noted it.

Likewise, these recipes were developed and tested using large eggs, 2% milk, freshly ground pepper, and fine sea salt unless otherwise noted. Throughout the book, you'll note that unsalted butter is called for; if you choose to use salted butter, please add less salt than specified in the recipe.

And finally, all recipes that use meat stocks were made using the recipes in the Basics section. If substituting purchased broths or stocks, please be very cautious when seasoning, since most commercial and deli-made preparations of this kind are very salty.

Spring recipes

Summer recipes

Autumn recipes

Winter recipes

Appetizers

Main Courses

Desserts

Basics

Stocks and Reductions

Vegetable Preparations

Savoury Preparations

Sweet Preparations

Savoury Sauces

Sweet Sauces and Toppings

Bringing It Together at Pangaea

When Peter Geary and I opened Pangaea in October 1996, our goal was to serve great-tasting food in an environment that was inclusive and comfortable but still stylish and fun. It took a lot of planning and sourcing to make our dream come true, but in the end, it seems to have worked out perfectly.

In 1996 sustainability had a much different meaning for most people than it does today. In fact, if you had stopped shoppers on Bay Street in front of the restaurant and asked them what sustainable food was, they might have answered freeze-drying or another preservation system as key to sustaining our food supply. Or, they may have pointed to science as the secret to making sure we all have enough to eat.

To be truthful, "sustainability" wasn't a word I used frequently myself in those days. Although I've always made conscious food choices, taste was king for me when I was a young chef, and even by the time Pangaea opened, I was highly aware that when you run a restaurant, your personal interests in eating locally grown food, raised responsibly,

have to be balanced with the realities of living not only in a northern climate, but also with the persistent economic constraints of being a restaurateur. As executive chef, my most important job is to find ingredients and manipulate them into menu items that please my conscience, my customers, *and* my accountant.

I spend a lot of my time seeking out the best-tasting ingredients I can so that I can satisfy these goals. As a result, sustainability is not a trend here at Pangaea but a path that I continue to travel with my customers and my suppliers. We aren't all the way there yet, but I've discovered that the fresh foods that are raised with the most integrity and that have travelled the least distance usually deliver exactly what I need to please palates.

That said, the modern food landscape is dotted with mountain-sized contradictions that can be difficult to scale. While farmers' market fare and sustainable food are more available at restaurants like Pangaea, agribusiness and mass-produced foods are also very prevalent in our society. On a smaller scale, similar contradictions affect me every day as I create order lists and menus for Pangaea. On the one hand, I want to cook like it's 1922, using unprocessed ingredients that need very little human intervention to be delicious. Simultaneously, the fantastic ingredients I'm offered from faraway countries intrigue me. My challenge is finding a sensible balance between these conflicting impulses and sources. In the end, I've decided that every ingredient we use has to have an intriguing or inspiring history. If there's nothing to say about an ingredient, it's likely not very good quality.

Looking into Our Bright Future

Since 1992, when I first became an executive chef responsible for creating menus, finding fantastic ingredients has been a daily challenge and an overwhelming pleasure. Over the years, I have created relationships with growers like David Cohlmeyer and foragers like Jonathan Forbes, who were willing to deliver their wares to my kitchen. These people have worked with me to grow and find the things I want on my menu, and our relationships have provided an enriching experience that ultimately has led me to write this book.

While I value the personal connections I've forged with so many of my suppliers, it takes a lot of time to manage all the orders, find new suppliers, and make sure I have what I need when I need it.

Over the years, as eating and cooking locally has become more fashionable, it's become easier to source local products and for me to make new connections. The Evergreen Brick Works Farmers' Market now has a chefs' market on Tuesday mornings where I can pick up produce, cheese, and specialty items from the Ontario greenbelt and meet local suppliers face-to-face. (To be honest, I often pop in there on my way to work just to have a coffee with chef friends who also shop at the market.)

Companies like 100km Foods Inc. have made my job easier, too. Started in 2007 by Paul Sawtell and Grace Mandarano, 100km Foods makes it easier for farmers and chefs to do business. They find farmers with great products, coordinate deliveries, and source new farms and products that chefs like me need to find to prepare our recipes. We haven't bought a lot of supplies from Paul and Grace because we've already developed so many great relationships, but if they'd been around in 1996 when Pangaea opened, my daily

quest for local produce with a story to tell would have been that much easier.

Another partnership that has brought great peace of mind to me and quality assurance to Pangaea diners is Ocean Wise. This Vancouver Aquarium program offers a meaningful action plan that helps chefs make environmentally responsible choices and ensure that their suppliers are credible and honourable. Ocean Wise not only provides information about what

fish are the best choices on any given day, but their team also works with restaurant suppliers to ensure that they are educated about sustainability.

Mike McDermid, manager of the Ocean Wise program, explains that "overfishing and habitat damage have led to massive species declines, even extinctions, and have caused dramatic shifts in ocean ecosystems. Within the past century, 90% of all large fish species are gone; we are now fishing the last 10%. The good

news is that chefs can help to reverse these trends by choosing seafood that is harvested in a sustainable manner."

We're happy to have Ocean Wise as advisers at the restaurant, and I'm happy to say that every fish and seafood recipe in this book falls within Ocean Wise guidelines, too.

Our Philosophy

Like many people, I've been duped by greenwashing; it's infuriating to find out that you've been fed a line when you felt you were making a considered choice. So, to avoid any confusion, let's be super clear: As I write this introduction, Pangaea is not a 100% green restaurant. Nor is it an exclusively organic or local-food restaurant. We are also not a 100% sustainable-food restaurant — but we're trying to get there, one forkful at a time!

What Pangaea is, is a place where wonderful fresh ingredients and creative recipes come together as good eating experiences. Similarly, this book encapsulates the stories that our favourite ingredients bring with them to our kitchen. While some of these tales are set in Toronto's backyard, others are set farther away on the Atlantic coast or even in Spain, where we've found food-producing practices that we admire and that create excellent-tasting ingredients that we think are special and deserve to be used. And that, in a nutshell, is why at Pangaea, everything tastes so good.

Pangaea Touchstones

Since before we opened the doors at Pangaea, we've used this list of words to describe our restaurant. Although we've been open for more than 14 years, we go back to this list on a daily basis to make sure the décor, food, service, and every other element of the Pangaea experience are consistent.

Simple
Understated
Elegant
Timeless
Thoughtful
Literary

Foragers and Farmers

Although we have dozens of suppliers who provide Pangaea with the wonderful ingredients we use to create our menu items, the four people below inspire us and teach us new things so often that I felt you just had to meet them.

Jonathan Forbes

When Jonathan Forbes started selling wild foods more than a decade ago, I was completely inspired by his resourcefulness. Instead of farming or looking for the next new fruit or vegetable to import from far-off lands, Jonathan used the rugged Ontario bush as a grocery store.

Angela Houpt

Fungi expert Angela Houpt spends her mornings tramping through damp fields and forests searching for wild mushrooms. Whether she turns up at our back door with a crate of delicate chanterelles or deeply creviced morels, she always knows everything about them. Her knowledge and enthusiasm for teaching are so great that after years of buying from Angela, almost every chef at Pangaea has become a bit of a mushroom expert, too.

David Cohlmeyer

Long before Canadian grocers and consumers were aware of organic and heirloom vegetables, David was growing such foods on his Cookstown farm, about 90 minutes north of Toronto. In fact, it was David making baby lettuces and heirloom variety tomatoes available to chefs that helped these items become household staples in Canadian homes.

Wanda Srdoc

When Wanda comes into the Pangaea kitchen and starts piling handfuls of fragrant white truffles onto her little pink scale, a circle of avid admirers in food-spattered aprons always forms around her. Flown in to Toronto immediately after they are picked on her family's land near Istria, Croatia, Wanda's truffles are consistently the best available in our city.

Front of the House

While I'm responsible for how the food tastes at Pangaea, my business partner, Peter Geary, strives to create a relaxed, elegant atmosphere in our dining room and at our bar so that our guests are ready to enjoy every morsel. On the following pages, he'll take you through Pangaea's service philosophy, since no one is better qualified to tell that story than the man who created it.

A warm welcome

Pangaea is our home away from home, so as you enter our front door we want you to be welcomed as though you're arriving at one of our houses.

Our goal is to make every guest feel that they're exactly where they should be; our goal is to help everyone relax and enjoy every moment at Pangaea. Whether you're the president of a multinational company, a couple out on a first date, a group of friends celebrating a special occasion, or a tired and hungry business traveller, Pangaea is for you.

While we always hate to say goodbye to our patrons at the end of a meal, I think the Pangaea "epilogue"— a warm word, help with your coat — makes the transition from our house to your house a little bit easier.

Our service philosophy

I once attended a dinner in England where a trolley with 39 cheeses was wheeled up to our table; it was an elegant, serious restaurant with a proud and earnest cheese sommelier who waxed lyrically about each cheese! By the time his seminar was concluded and our order

was taken, 25 minutes had disappeared. Needless to say, by that time we'd completely lost the thread of our conversation.

At Pangaea, we approach things a little differently. Sure our wine list is impressive. Yes, every ingredient on your plate has a story. And of course every piece of art in the restaurant was commissioned for the space. But unless our patrons initiate conversations about these elements of the Pangaea experience, we'll just strive to serve our patrons deftly and make sure they have everything they need. Because sometimes, with full service, less can be more.

At our bar

I grew up in England at a time when the public house, or the "pub," was — along with the church, the village hall, and the post office — one of the primary social hubs of the community. Neighbours congregated there in a warm, welcoming, informal setting, striking up friendly conversations with anyone within earshot. While it's a more elegant setting than my neighbourhood pub back in England, Pangaea's cozy bar is similarly friendly. It differs only in that the wine selection is award-winning and the floors are polished maple instead of sticky old carpet.

Besides our regular after-work bar customers — many of whom have become friends as they sipped their evening glasses of wine — our bar is a place where single diners, male and female, feel comfortable. It's a place where stimulating conversation is as common as a good joke and where, if people don't know your name when you arrive, they likely will by the time you leave.

Wine at Pangaea

Our attitude about wine is like our outlook on life: the glass should always be half full.

Over the years, we've worked diligently to build an extensive, well-rounded wine list, which has been acknowledged both locally with the VQA (Vintners Quality Alliance) Award of Excellence and internationally by the *Wine Spectator* magazine "Best of the Best" Wine List Award. And while we're very proud of these accomplishments, our core philosophy at Pangaea is that wine — and food, for that matter — should be fun!

As a result, our wine list and wine service, like the restaurant itself, are approachable and friendly. I love it when guests ask us to recommend a wine to complement a particular dish or tell us that they really want to try something new. With hundreds of bottles to choose from, there's always something in our cellar for every palate and budget.

And like the suppliers who bring Martin and his crew wonderful ingredients, we make an effort to know as many of the winemakers featured on our list as possible. So when we get guests who want to chat about wine, we're ready, willing, and able.

*Clive Coates, pictured left, led a tutored Burgundy Wine tasting at Pangaea, April 23, 2008.

Behind the Kitchen Door

Not always as polished and suave as our front-of-house staff, but every bit as important, are the cooks who work long hours behind the scenes. Since workspace is at a premium in our kitchen, everyone needs to be efficient and respectful of one another's turf. While I'm not going to say that our tempers never reach a flashpoint, I'm proud to say that our kitchen is nothing like the ones you see on reality TV shows. In fact, although our senior staff often tell junior staff the unvarnished truth about their work, it's always done with a context and is designed to improve not just the Pangaea experience but also each team member's skills.

Like every ingredient that comes through our back door, each cook at Pangaea has a story and experiences that make our food taste better. While chef de cuisine Derek Bendig, pastry chef Colen Quinn, and sous chefs Andrew Fawcett, Christopher Waye and Rob Clarke contribute the most creativity, we give all a chance to voice their ideas. If they match our core values (see page 21), even an apprentice's idea just might make it onto the menu.

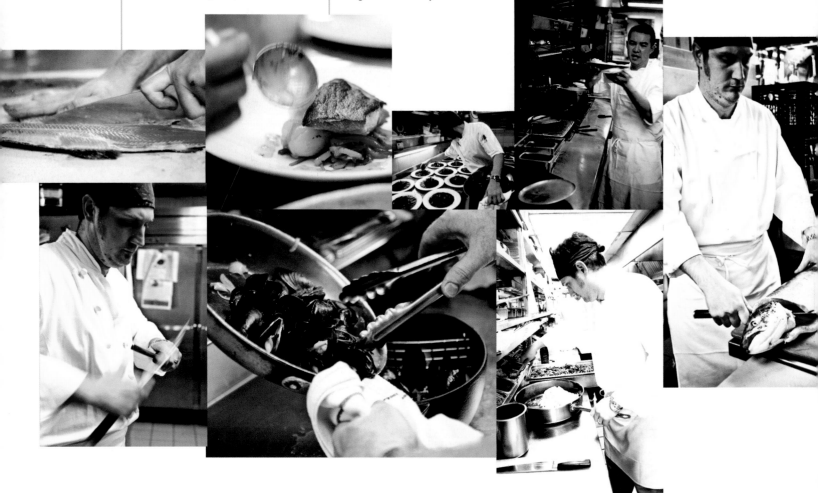

The Team

Our restaurant's namesake, the super continent Pangaea, broke apart 180 million years ago because the tectonic plates beneath its lush, green surface kept shifting and heaving.

Plates are always on the move at Pangaea restaurant, too. Our servers gingerly transport artfully composed plates of fresh, delicious food to each table and then later, ferry the emptied plates back to the kitchen to be washed. In between, they fill and refill glasses and consult on wine choices and explain our menu items to anyone who wants to learn about why everything at Pangaea tastes so very good. They're busy! Yet somehow they seem to have fun while they're doing it.

Teaching

I'm a dying breed. Seriously, it's true. When I chose to become a chef, many hotels and some restaurants still offered comprehensive apprenticeship programs that prepared cooks to write the tests required to become papered chefs. I started my culinary education at the Westin Hotel in Ottawa, where I was mentored, under a team of seasoned professionals, through each kitchen department to learn not only the basics but also the finer points of cooking.

Today, those opportunities are pretty much non-existent here in Canada. Instead, the only route open to most people who aspire to become well-rounded chefs, qualified to pass a red seal exam, is to go to culinary school and then work the necessary hours to qualify as a candidate for the test. It's a good system but not the same as the Old World–inspired mentorship I experienced.

I try to teach daily at Pangaea, sharing techniques and training palates. As a result, our kitchen is often crowded with students and apprentices who are eager to learn from not only me but also our other senior staff members.

Likewise, several times a term, I also teach at Humber College so that I can pay back my profession by helping young cooks succeed and thrive in this difficult but ultimately rewarding profession. I love it!

Spring

Foraged Foods

While most if not all of you have purchased food in a grocery store and visited a farm to buy ingredients, I doubt that many of you have gone for a walk in the woods or a meadow and come home with a pocketful of ingredients to use in your dinner. But this is exactly what many of our most cherished suppliers do. They forage in wild spaces for delicious ingredients that you just can't buy at a store in any form.

One of these suppliers is Jonathan Forbes, who brings us many native foods that inspire us. When we first met a decade or so ago, I intended only to buy ramps and mushrooms from him. Soon I learned about Jonathan's other Ontario treasures, such as wild asparagus, cattail hearts, and the wonderful caper-style pickles he makes from very young milkweed pods, marsh marigold buds, and ox-eye daisies (which are different from Shasta daisies in

that they spread quickly by producing runners).

I love working with Jonathan because he really understands sustainability and always picks responsibly so that wild areas remain abundantly populated. "Since milkweed pods and ox-eye daisies are invasive plants that generally cover large areas, they are hard to harm," he notes. "However, my rule of thumb is to harvest no more than 15% of the

available plants you find in the wild."

While ox-eye daisy buds can be harvested from the flowers in a garden, Jonathan depends on wild sources for the milkweed and marsh marigold buds that he brines and bottles for chefs like me. Picking the buds to make capers is a difficult job that must be done quickly and by hand. Each flower bud has to be very small and tightly compacted, which means there is only a week-long window of opportunity for picking and preparation. Milkweed pods are slightly more forgiving since they can be picked when they are as small as buds and up to as long as 1½-inches (3 cm).

Milkweed pods are quite mild and will take on the flavours of their brine nicely. At Pangaea we use them to garnish charcuterie platters. Ox-eye daisy capers have a distinct floral flavour, and although they are much sweeter than traditional capers, we find they still make a great garnish for the ocean trout we cold-smoke.

We use ramps and wild leeks to make not only lovely, bright reen soups like the one on page 49 but also as a grilled vegetable to accompany seafood. Meanwhile, we treat cattail hearts like white asparagus and serve them along with all kinds of springtime entrées.

The Magic of Mushrooms

Each spring, the first morels are cause for celebration in the Pangaea kitchen. The emergence of these honeycomb-textured mushrooms from the cold Ontario ground heralds the return not only of lengthening days and warmer weather but also of abundant local produce. As a chef, my favourite thing about morels is their wonderfully deep, woodsy flavour, which helps your palate transition from cold-weather foods to lighter, fresher-tasting summer foods.

We buy morels each spring from a number of foragers, including Angela Houpt and Jonathan Forbes (see page 22). Unlike other species of mushrooms, morels cannot be domesticated, so a plentiful crop one year does not mean that they can be found in the same area again the next. In fact, that morels are so elusive gives them some of their cachet among gourmets and causes prices to fluctuate wildly each year depending on the luck foragers have in the woods. Angela tells me that morels fruit most abundantly on ground that has been recently cleared or burned — construction sites can be good places to find them — and in elm stands and fruit orchards, but I've only found them in the woods.

Like truffles, morels belong to the category of fungus called the Ascomycetes, which do not have gills or pores like many other mushrooms. Sometimes called sponge mushrooms, morels are cone-shaped, with deep, wavy ridges that traverse their length.

The stem ends can be quite tough, and each mushroom has an inner cavity that can trap hot sauces, so I always remind our servers to warn Pangaea customers to be careful when they take a bite of a morel since it may contain a shockingly hot surprise!

Always avoid morels whose caps are soft or mushy, or mushrooms that become granular when rubbed with your thumb, because these are signs that the morels are old and potentially wormy. Because of the irregular shape of the surface of morels, they cannot be cleaned easily even when rubbed or brushed. I avoid soaking morels in water since, like raspberries, even brief soaking diminishes their flavour and damages their texture. If the morels you buy are gritty or dirty, cut them in half lengthwise and rinse them quickly under cold running water. Then blot them on paper towels and cook immediately.

Besides the recipes I've included in this book, there are hundreds of other ways to prepare morels. Just be sure to cook them thoroughly. Although button and many other mushrooms can be sliced and added raw to salads, morels contain a chemical called monomethylhydrazine (MMH) that can cause acute illness, especially if the raw morels are ingested with a glass of wine or other alcohol.

Making Wiser Choices

As you might remember from reading the introduction — you did read it, didn't you? — all the fish and seafood we serve at Pangaea conform to guidelines created by the Vancouver Aquarium that ensure that only the most sustainable fish and seafood are delivered to our kitchen door.

Before I made my commitment to Ocean Wise, I had been a member of other organizations such as the Endangered Fish Alliance and Seafood Watch. Like Ocean Wise, these organizations were born of a belief that restaurant and hotel chefs could make a difference in the world by choosing only fish and seafood that are sustainable and caught without harming other species or habitats. Their mandates were great in theory; however, in practice it meant that as an already busy restaurateur I needed to quiz my suppliers on a daily basis so that I could evaluate my choices.

Then along came Ocean Wise. They make it so easy for chefs like me to offer sustainable fish and seafood options. Their team works with us to find suppliers that offer what we need and can verify that what's being shipped to the restaurant is indeed sustainable.

Buh-bye Shrimp, Hello Spot Prawns!

Shrimp are one of the most appealing shellfish. Like the Pangaea landmass that broke apart 150 million years ago and united all lands, shrimp seems to bridge gaps, too. Even people who don't care for other fish and seafood still like shrimp. So it isn't surprising to me, when I look back over the many menus I've written for both Pangaea and the restaurants I worked at before Peter and I went into business, to see that shrimp has always had a prominent place on my menus.

In 2008, when I met Mike McDermid from the Vancouver Aquarium's Ocean Wise program, I was shocked to learn that the abundance of shrimp we were selling was not good for the oceans. It turns out that many of the methods used to gather shrimp harm other species in the process. Fortunately, Mike had a wonderful solution for us: British Columbian spot prawns.

Prawns are similar to shrimp in many ways. Some people dismiss the word "prawn" as a marketing term for a large shrimp and define a prawn as a freshwater shrimp species; however, the website for BC seafood defines spot prawns as the largest of the seven commercial species of shrimp found in Canada's western coastal waters. I've found they are pretty consistently sized at 16 to 20 pieces per pound. It turns out that this sustainable alternative to the shrimp is also absolutely delicious. Not only is the flesh crunchy and very sweet, but the shells also make a fantastic broth to use in bisque and sauces.

The biggest challenge about using spot prawns on a menu in Toronto is that they are highly perishable. To run a large restaurant like Pangaea, we need a steady supply and ample warning when availability isn't reliable. So we reached out to fisherman Steve Johansen, who owns Organic Ocean. I call him on his cellphone while he's on the water setting and retrieving his Ocean Wise–approved traps so that I know what he's going to be able to send to Pangaea later that day.

Unfortunately, the spot prawn season is very short, only about eight weeks during May and June, so we're left with 10 months of the year when our patrons are still hungry for shrimp. The great news is that every day more suppliers are realizing the need to use sustainable methods and we now have a new Nova Scotia supplier who will be selling us sustainable Atlantic shrimp soon.

Spring
recipes

Appetizers

Main Courses

Desserts

Triptych of Spring Soups
White Asparagus with Parmesan Crisp
Wild Mushroom
Wild Leek and Fava Bean with Orange Foam

Seasonal

soup purées showcasing the freshest ingredients in our kitchen are featured in trios every day on our menu. This trio, featuring organic vegetables and foraged wild springtime treasures, is one of my favourite spring combinations. We serve these trios in small cups nestled on a larger platter so that patrons can enjoy them separately or mix them up as they like.

For vegetarian versions, you can substitute water for the chicken stock.

Note

You should also know that we use a high-powered Vita-Mix blender to create an absolutely silky soup purée. If you don't have a good-quality blender, strain the soups to ensure they are smooth.

For 8 servings each of three soups

White Asparagus Soup

1 tbsp (15 mL) butter
2 cups (500 mL) trimmed, peeled, chopped white asparagus
1/4 cup (60 mL) chopped onion
1 tsp (5 mL) chopped garlic
2 tbsp (30 mL) all-purpose flour
1/2 cup (125 mL) white wine
1 tsp (5 mL) lemon juice
2 1/4 cups (550 mL) chicken stock (see page 208)
1 bay leaf
1/2 tsp (2 mL) salt or to taste

Parmesan Crisp

1/2 cup (125 mL) grated Grano Padano or Reggiano cheese

To Serve

Warm three small bowls per person. Spoon out even portions of the three soups and garnish with appropriate toppings.

Tips

If a soup thickens as it sits, adjust the texture by adding a little boiling water.

For vegetarian versions, substitute vegetable broth or water for the chicken stock.

White Asparagus Soup

In a large saucepan set over medium heat, melt the butter. Once it foams, add the asparagus, onion, and garlic. Cook, stirring constantly, for 5 minutes or until the vegetables soften slightly. Dust the asparagus mixture with the flour and mix together well.

Stir in the white wine, lemon juice, chicken stock, bay leaf, and salt; bring to a boil. Reduce heat to a simmer and cook for 20 minutes; remove from heat and season to taste.

Cool slightly. Purée the soup in a high-speed blender. Pass the mixture through a medium strainer. Taste and adjust salt, if necessary.

Parmesan Crisp

Preheat oven to 325°F (160°C). On a silicon mat–lined baking sheet, sprinkle the cheese into 8 loose, thin piles. Bake until slightly golden brown. Cool completely; remove gently from sheets.

Wild Mushroom Soup

2 tbsp (30 mL) butter
1/4 cup (60 mL) chopped onion
1 tsp (5 mL) chopped garlic
5 cups (1.25 L) chopped, trimmed mixed wild mushrooms, such as chanterelles, hedgehogs, morels, shiitake, etc.
1/4 cup (60 mL) brandy
1/4 cup (60 mL) white wine
2 1/2 cups (625 mL) chicken stock (see page 208)
1 tsp (5 mL) chopped fresh thyme leaves
1/2 tsp (2 mL) salt or to taste

Garnish

1 tsp (5 mL) unsalted butter
8 small mushroom caps
Salt to taste

Wild Mushroom Soup

In a large saucepan set over medium heat, melt the butter. Once it foams, add the onions and garlic. Cook, stirring often, until you can smell the garlic caramelizing, about 3 minutes. Add the mushrooms and stir well. Stir in the brandy and white wine; bring to a boil; reduce the liquid until you can see the bottom of the pan when you stir the mixture. Add the chicken stock and fresh thyme leaves; bring to a boil. Reduce the heat and simmer for 15 minutes.

Remove from heat and cool slightly. Purée the soup in a high-speed blender. Pass the mixture through a medium strainer. Taste and adjust salt, if necessary.

Garnish

In a small skillet set over medium heat, melt the butter. Add the mushroom caps and cook, turning often, for 3 minutes or until fork tender but not browned. Season to taste. Reserve at room temperature to float, gill sides up, on soup before serving.

Wild Leek and Fava Bean Soup
1 tbsp (15 mL) butter
¼ cup (60 mL) chopped onion
¼ cup (60 mL) pancetta, diced
2 cups (500 mL) parboiled, peeled fresh
    fava beans
3 cups (750 mL) chicken stock (see page 208)
½ cup (125 mL) washed, trimmed, chopped
    ramps (wild leeks)
1 tbsp (15 mL) chopped mint
½ tsp (2 mL) salt or to taste

Orange Foam
½ cup (125 mL) whole (homogenized) milk
1½ tsp (7 mL) finely grated orange zest

Wild Leek and Fava Bean Soup
In a large saucepan set over medium heat,
melt the butter. Once it foams, add the onions
and pancetta. Cook, stirring constantly, for 5
minutes or until the vegetables soften slightly
but do not change colour. Add the beans and
chicken stock; bring to a boil. Simmer for 10
minutes or until beans are tender. Add the
ramps and cook for 1 minute. Stir in the mint
and salt.

Remove from heat and cool slightly. Purée
the soup in a high-speed blender. Pass the
mixture through a medium strainer. Taste
and adjust salt, if necessary.

Orange Foam
Just before serving the soups, place the milk
in a 1 cup (250 mL) metal pitcher; add the
orange zest. Use the steamer wand from a
cappuccino machine to create a light and
frothy foam.

Soft-Shell Crab Salad
with Watermelon, Avocado,
Arugula, and Herb Oil

Soft-Shell Crab Salad
with Watermelon, Avocado,
Arugula, and Herb Oil

Soft-shell

crab season is short, usually lasting only from the first full moon in May to July. From then, the steady supply is over and we get only sporadic shipments of this delicious seafood until September, when the season is officially over.

Spring is the time of year when blue crabs have a growth spurt. As their shells expand, they molt, leaving just a soft skeletal covering for a few days as the new, bigger shell develops. It's during this short window of time that soft-shell crabs can be harvested and eaten whole.

The best soft-shell crabs come from Chesapeake Bay, but there are edible soft-shell crabs in the Gulf of Mexico, too. To make sure the crabs can stay alive until cooking, buy them packed in a crate of straw-covered ice; this will keep them very cold and dormant but ensure they don't freeze.

A word of warning: If you make soft-shell crabs for a dinner party, discreetly and gently warn your guests that they will be eating a whole crab before they arrive. We forgot that important step one time and ended up embarrassing one of our friends who wasn't up for the experience. To make a long story short, broken china ensued!

Herb Oil
Bring a large saucepan of salted water to a boil. Immerse the parsley in the water and immediately strain. Plunge the hot parsley into ice water and cool completely. Drain well and dry on paper towel.

Combine the blanched parsley and fresh herbs in a blender. Pour in the oil and purée to form a smooth paste. Line a mesh sieve with cheesecloth and suspend over a bowl. Scrape the blended paste into the cheesecloth-lined sieve and tie the ends of the cheesecloth to enclose mixture tightly. Suspend this herb bundle over the bowl, using the tail of a wooden spoon or chopsticks as a cross-support; set in the refrigerator to drain overnight.

Discard the herb bundle and reserve the collected oil, but do not squeeze the cheesecloth (it will make the oil cloudy). Herb oil can be covered tightly and kept in the refrigerator for up to 3 days.

Salad
Peel the watermelon and cut off the two rounded ends. Slice the remaining watermelon thinly and cut each piece into wedges to make 18 wedges in total.

On six plates, layer 3 watermelon wedges and equal amounts of avocado, arugula, parsley, chervil, and chives. Keep chilled.

Soft-Shell Crabs
Using kitchen shears, cut off the front of each crab directly behind the eyes. Lift up the left side of the shell and pull out the feathery gills; repeat on the other side. Flip the crab over and trim off the tail. Rinse under cold water and pat dry with a paper towel. Place the egg whites in a medium bowl, whip until frothy, and set aside. In a large, shallow bowl, combine the flour and piment d'espelette and set aside.

Heat the oil in a large skillet set over medium-high heat. Dip the soft-shell crabs into the egg whites to coat well. Next dip the crabs in the flour until well coated on each side; shake off any excess flour and place the crabs, back-side down, in the hot skillet. Sear on both sides until golden brown. Transfer to a paper towel–lined baking sheet, season with salt and pepper, and keep warm in a 150°F (65°C) oven.

To Assemble
Place a crab on top of the salad. Drizzle herb oil around each stack, and add a few drops of balsamic vinegar.

For 6 servings

Herb Oil
3 cups (750 mL) lightly packed fresh parsley leaves
1 cup (250 mL) lightly packed fresh chervil leaves
$1/2$ cup (125 mL) lightly packed fresh tarragon leaves
$1/2$ cup (125 mL) lightly packed fresh chives
1 cup (250 mL) grapeseed oil

Salad
$1/2$ baby seedless watermelon
2 avocados, halved, pitted, peeled, and sliced
2 cups (500 mL) lightly packed fresh arugula leaves
$1/4$ cup (60 mL) lightly packed fresh parsley leaves
$1/4$ cup (60 mL) lightly packed fresh chervil leaves
$1/4$ cup (60 mL) 1-inch (2.5 cm) fresh chives lengths
1 tsp (5 mL) balsamic vinegar

Soft-Shell Crabs
6 jumbo (4.5 oz/130 g each) or whale (5.9 oz/165 g each) soft-shell crabs
3 egg whites, beaten
2 cups (500 mL) all-purpose flour
3 tbsp (45 mL) freshly ground piment d'espelette (see note on page 92) or hot Spanish paprika
2 tbsp (30 mL) canola oil
Salt and pepper to taste

Russian and Iranian caviar have become so famous that it's hard to believe Canada used to be one of the number-one producers of this delicacy.

Until almost the end of the 19th century, the waterways of Ontario's Lake of the Woods were teeming with sturgeon. Regrettably, overfishing and paper mill pollution decimated the population. Since the 1970s, initiatives to rehabilitate these waterways have been ongoing, and now caviar from Rainy River and Lake Abitibi are becoming more available to restaurants; however, at this time, only very small quantities are available.

I wish that the case were different, since when our chefs did an in-house caviar tasting, the Canadian Abitibi roe came in third (the German and French were our first and second choices) before the better-known Russian and Iranian osetra varieties. Hopefully, in time, production will increase so that Canada can reestablish its reputation as a leading caviar producer.

One seafood species that we have managed well is spot prawns. As I described on page 43, they are a Canadian ocean-management success story!

Spot Prawns

Separate the bodies and tails of the spot prawns from the heads; discard heads. Peel to the tailfan. Slit down the backs of the prawns to butterfly, then remove and discard the long, fine filaments that are the digestive tracts. Place cleaned prawns on paper towels and refrigerate until needed.

Green and White Asparagus

For the white asparagus, peel the bottom three-quarters and trim off 1 inch (2.5 cm) of each stem. Place cleaned stalks in a pot that has enough room to allow them to lie flat but fit snugly. Fill pot with 4 cups (1 L) of water; add the lemon juice and half of the salt. Bring to a boil and then reduce to a simmer; cook for 5 minutes. Remove from heat and allow asparagus to cool in the cooking liquid for 15 minutes. Drain well.

To prepare the green asparagus, peel the bottom three-quarters and trim the tough ends. In a large pot, bring 8 cups (2 L) of water to a boil; add the remaining salt. Plunge the asparagus into the water and blanch for 2 minutes. Plunge the asparagus into ice water to stop the cooking. Let stand for 5 minutes or until thoroughly chilled; drain well.

Trim all the cooked asparagus so that stalks are the same length (the trimmed ends can be reserved for another use, such as making a salad).

Olive Oil Béarnaise Sauce

Remove the leaves from the tarragon sprigs and chop finely. Measure out 1 tbsp (15 mL) and reserve separately from stems.

In a small saucepan set over medium heat, melt the butter. Add the shallots and sauté for 1 minute or until translucent; stir in the garlic and pepper. Cook for 30 seconds. Add the white wine, white wine vinegar, and lemon juice. Stir in the reserved tarragon stems. Simmer gently for about 15 minutes or until the liquid is reduced by about three-quarters. Strain this mixture through a fine sieve; cool to room temperature.

Place the egg yolks in a medium-sized heatproof bowl, or the top of a double boiler; place over a pot one-third full of barely simmering water. Whisk the egg yolks for 30 seconds and remove from heat to cool; return to heat and continue to beat, pausing at similar intervals, for 2 minutes or until eggs are pale and hold a ribbon when the whisk is lifted from the bowl.

Add the cooled wine reduction and whisk over the barely simmering water for 3 minutes or until thick enough that the bottom of the bowl is visible between whisk strokes and the temperature of the mixture registers 105°F (40°C) on an instant-read thermometer.

For 6 servings

18 spot prawns

Green and White Asparagus
18 white asparagus stalks
12 cups (3 L) water, divided
1 lemon, zested and juiced
4 tsp (20 mL) salt, divided
18 green asparagus stalks

Olive Oil Béarnaise Sauce
4 sprigs fresh tarragon (approx.)
1 tsp (5 mL) butter
2 tbsp (30 mL) minced shallot
1/2 tsp (2 mL) minced garlic
Pinch freshly ground black pepper (approx.)
1/2 cup (125 mL) white wine
1/4 cup (60 mL) white wine vinegar
1/4 tsp (1 mL) freshly squeezed lemon juice
4 egg yolks
1/4 cup (60 mL) extra virgin olive oil
1/4 tsp (1 mL) salt
Pinch cayenne pepper

Garnish
2 tbsp (30 mL) Abitibi caviar or other sustainably sourced fish eggs
Fresh chervil or parsley leaves

Spot Prawns
on Green and White Asparagus,
Olive Oil Béarnaise Sauce,
Abitibi Caviar, and Chervil

Transfer the bowl to the counter. Place a damp cloth under the bowl to hold it still. Still whisking, slowly drizzle in the oil until the mixture is very thick and creamy. Whisk in salt and cayenne. Fold in reserved tarragon leaves. Let stand at room temperature for up to 15 minutes.

To Assemble
Preheat your oven's broiler. On a heatproof platter or six individual heatproof plates, alternately arrange green and white asparagus with their tips pointing in the same direction. Place under the broiler to remove the chill from the asparagus. Ladle a little béarnaise down the centre of the asparagus and arrange the prawns over the sauce. Place the plate under the broiler and glaze for 20 to 30 seconds or until the prawns are opaque and the sauce is lightly browned. Place a small dollop of caviar on each shrimp and garnish with chervil. Serve immediately.

Charcuterie

Cured meats, from prosciutto to chorizo to

headcheese, are a specialty of the Pangaea kitchen. While teaching you to make your own charcuterie would be fun, the task exceeds the scope of this book. Instead, I'll give you a few guidelines about buying charcuterie as well as a couple of recipes for the fresh pickles we make to accompany our artisan-cured meats.

I've added aging time in these pickle recipes, but at the restaurant we Cryovac (vacuum seal) them, which allows them to cure more quickly so we can serve them the next day!

Turmeric Cauliflower

2 cups (500 mL) white wine vinegar
1 cup (250 mL) turbinado sugar
1 ½ tsp (7 mL) turmeric
1 tsp (5 mL) whole black peppercorns
2 bay leaves
1 orange
2 cups (500 mL) cauliflower, separated
    into small florets

Crunchy Dill Pickles

3 cups (750 mL) water
3 cups (750 mL) white vinegar
¼ cup (60 mL) granulated sugar
1 tbsp (15 mL) kosher salt
2 cloves garlic, sliced
4 crowns fresh dill
1 tbsp (15 mL) dried dill seeds
2 tsp (10 mL) whole black peppercorns
5 lbs (2.5 kg) baby cucumbers, washed
    and cut into quarters

Turmeric Cauliflower

Place the vinegar, sugar, turmeric, peppercorns, and bay leaves in an 8-cup (2 L) saucepan. Peel the orange using a vegetable peeler, being careful to avoid the white pith. Add the peel to the vinegar mixture and bring to a boil; simmer for 5 minutes. Add cauliflower and simmer for 2 minutes. Ladle hot ingredients into sterilized canning jars and secure with sterilized lids and rings. Once fully cooled, store jars in the refrigerator for at least 3 days and for up to 3 weeks.

Crunchy Dill Pickles

Place the water, vinegar, sugar, salt, garlic, dill, dill seeds, and peppercorns into a 16-cup (4 L) saucepan; bring to boil. Reduce heat and simmer for 5 minutes. Remove from heat and cool completely. Pack the quartered baby cucumbers into sterilized jars and cover completely with pickling liquid. Cover tightly and refrigerate for 1 week before use.

Creating a Great Charcuterie Platter

- Ideally, buy charcuterie from a company that makes it themselves.
- Gently squeeze dry-cured sausages. When properly made and cured, sausages should be compact and firm.
- Ask the store to cut open a sausage so you can see what it looks like inside:
  - The fat particles inside should look uniformly white.
  - If there are gaps or holes inside, you know the sausage wasn't properly packed and is unsafe to eat.
  - If the sausage is more visibly dry around the edges, you know it wasn't cured in a humidity-controlled environment.

Grilled Asian-Glazed Quail
with Crisp Tempura Onion Rings

Great recipes

sometimes have humble beginnings; such is the case with this recipe. In the early 1990s, when I worked at Pronto — before I even became executive chef there — the cooks were in mad competition to create the perfect chicken wings. We all took turns showing off our inspirations, and the results were consumed and voted upon at the nightly staff meal the cooks shared with the servers.

This marinade was a huge hit on chicken wings, so I thought, why not try it on quail? And guess what? It was even better on that succulent, dark-meat bird than on milder-tasting chicken.

For 6 servings

Asian-Glazed Quail
1/4 cup (60 mL) soy sauce
2 tbsp (30 mL) Demerara or raw sugar
1 tsp (5 mL) toasted sesame oil
1 tsp (5 mL) minced garlic
6 extra-large quails
2 cups (500 mL) mizuna or other
    salad greens
1/2 tsp (2 mL) lime juice
1/3 cup (75 mL) chicken reduction
    (see page 209)
6 tbsp (90 mL) Maple-Chile Sauce
    (see page 110)

Tempura Onion Rings
1 large Vidalia onion
1 cup (250 mL) all-purpose flour, divided
1 egg yolk
1 cup (250 mL) cold sparkling mineral water
1/2 tsp (2 mL) salt
Pinch freshly ground white pepper
1 ice cube

Quail
In a saucepan, combine the soy sauce, sugar, sesame oil, and garlic. Place over medium-high heat and bring to a boil. Reduce the heat and simmer for 5 minutes, stirring occasionally. Cool, stirring occasionally.

Meanwhile, use a boning knife to remove the neck and wing tips from each quail. Next, with each quail on its back, start at the breastbone and slice between the bones and the flesh. Bisect the quail lengthwise. Twist the legs and wings free at their joints, but leave the leg and the breast attached by the skin. Pinch the bottom of the larger leg bone. Use your fingers to push up the meat to the first joint; remove the bone with a twisting action, leaving only the smaller bone still in the leg. Place the quail halves in a medium bowl; toss the quail in just enough of the marinade to coat evenly. Cover and refrigerate for at least 2 hours or for up to 24 hours.

Preheat the grill or a grill pan over medium-high heat. Grease the grate or pan well. Grill the quail for about 2 minutes per side or until the skin is a mahogany colour but the meat is cooked to no more than medium doneness.

Tempura Onion Rings
Prepare and preheat the deep fryer to 360°F (185°C) according to the manufacturer's instructions.

Meanwhile, peel the onion and slice 1/4 inch (6 mm) thick. Separate into individual rings. Choose the largest ones (you'll need at least 12) and dust lightly with 1/3 cup (75 mL) of the flour. Reserve the remaining onions for another use.

In a medium bowl, whisk together the egg and water. Blend in the remaining 2/3 cup (150 mL) of flour, the salt and white pepper; whisk until smooth. Stir in the ice cube.

Drop the flour-dusted onion rings into the batter. Turn to coat all over. Carefully lower 4 to 5 onion rings into the hot oil without splashing; fry for 1 1/2 minutes per side, making sure that the rings stay separated to prevent sticking.

When batter is just slightly coloured, remove the rings from the oil; drain on paper towels. Season lightly with salt. Keep warm.

To Assemble
Stack 2 onion rings on a large plate. Gather the ends of the greens together to make six equal-sized bouquets. Trim ends if necessary to make them about the same length. Stand one bunch in the centre of each onion ring stack. Drizzle a few drops of lime juice over the greens. Drizzle the plate with the chicken reduction. Place 2 quail halves, with the legs pointing outward, on the plate. Serve the Maple-Chile Sauce on the side.

Tip
If you are a confident deep-fryer, you can add great texture and even more crunch to your onion rings by drizzling a little extra batter over each onion ring while it fries in the oil. You get the most control by using your fingertips, but if you're a tidy sort, drizzle the batter from a teaspoon.

Sunchokes

are a root vegetable I've been encouraging people to try for more than 15 years. This knobby tuber comes in many sizes, but I choose the ones that look like fingerling potatoes. They have a sweet, crunchy appeal and roast up a lot like a potato but have a much lighter texture. Also called Jerusalem artichokes, sunchokes aren't part of the artichoke family; they're actually a type of sunflower. Because this tuber has so much natural moisture, sunchokes should be handled carefully to prevent bruising; likewise, withered or wrinkled sunchokes should be discarded.

While Atlantic cod is sadly overfished and compromised as a population, Alaskan black cod caught by bottom longline, trap, or hook and line is a sustainable seafood choice that tastes fantastic! As you can see, I treat this white, firm fish like meat, even creating a meat-infused sauce to complement the earthy mushrooms and herbs used in the vegetables, so feel free to serve it with a light, fruity pinot noir or other red wine.

For 6 servings

Black Cod
6 Alaskan black cod fillets, about 2 lbs (1 kg) in total
1/2 tsp (2 mL) salt
1/2 tsp (2 mL) freshly ground black pepper
1 tbsp (15 mL) canola oil (approx.)

Sauce
1 cup (250 mL) veal reduction (see page 210)
1 tsp (5 mL) chopped fresh thyme leaves
1 tbsp (15 mL) chopped fresh parsley leaves
2 tbsp (30 mL) cold butter, cubed
Pinch salt or to taste
Pinch freshly ground black pepper or to taste
1 tsp (5 mL) minced black summer truffle trimmings or 6 drops Wanda's truffle oil

Garnish
6 thin round slices pancetta
1 tsp (5 mL) butter
6 sprigs fresh thyme

Vegetables
8 sunchokes, about 2 cups (500 mL)
1/4 cup (60 mL) canola oil, divided
1/2 tsp (2 mL) salt or to taste
3 cups (750 mL) fresh morels or other mushrooms
1 shallot, minced
1/4 cup (60 mL) dry white wine
2 cloves garlic, minced
1 tsp (5 mL) freshly squeezed lemon juice
Salt and freshly ground black pepper to taste
1 tsp (5 mL) butter
1 cup (250 mL) halved cherry tomatoes
3 cups (750 mL) lightly packed baby spinach leaves

Black Cod
Preheat the oven to 350°F (180°C). Set a large, heavy, ovenproof skillet over high heat. Season the cod evenly with salt and pepper. When the pan is very hot, add 1 tbsp (15 mL) of oil. Add three pieces of cod, skin-side down, and sear for 2 minutes per side. Remove and reserve on a warm platter. Sear the remaining fillets, adding a little more oil if necessary, then return all the browned fish to the skillet, arranging it flesh-side down in one layer. Transfer skillet to the oven and cook for 5 minutes or until the fish flakes easily when tested with a fork. Remove from the hot pan immediately and keep warm. Leave the oven on at 350°F (180°C).

Sauce
Meanwhile, in a saucepan set over medium-high heat, combine the veal reduction, thyme, and parsley and bring to a boil. Reduce heat to low and simmer, stirring occasionally, for 5 minutes. Remove from heat. Whisk in the cold butter cubes, adding just a little at a time, until sauce is slightly thickened and all the butter is incorporated. Season with salt and pepper to taste. Keep warm. Whisk in the black truffles or truffle oil just before assembling the dish.

Garnish
Place the pancetta on a parchment paper–lined baking sheet and roast in the preheated oven for 10 minutes or until crisp. Remove from tray and transfer to paper towel–lined tray. Keep warm. Just before assembling the plates, place a sprig of thyme through the naturally formed hole in the centre of each circle of the pancetta and use to garnish the plate.

Vegetables
Turn up the oven to 375°F (190°C). Wash the sunchokes thoroughly, leaving skin on. Pat dry and cut each sunchoke in half lengthwise. Toss with 1 tbsp (15 mL) of the oil to coat evenly. Season lightly with salt. Spread the sunchokes, cut-side down, evenly on a baking sheet; roast on the middle rack for 30 minutes, turning halfway through. Remove from oven and cover with foil to keep warm.

Meanwhile, trim the stem ends from the mushrooms using a sharp paring knife. Brush and shake any loose mulch or dirt from the morel caps and stems.

Heat the remaining oil in a clean skillet; add the shallots and mushrooms. Cook, tossing, until you notice the stems of the mushrooms begin to brown. Once the mushrooms are golden, deglaze the pan with white wine. Stir in the garlic. Reduce the pan juices until the mushrooms are glazed. Add the lemon juice and season with salt and pepper to taste. Transfer to a heated bowl and keep warm.

Wipe out the warm skillet to remove any brown bits. Add the butter and return the skillet to the heat. Once the butter foams, toss in the cherry tomatoes and reserved sunchokes and mushrooms. Heat through

Black Cod
with Roasted Sunchokes,
Pancetta, Wild Mushrooms,
Baby Spinach, and Truffle Jus

and add the spinach. Toss until greens just begin to wilt. Taste and add additional salt and pepper if necessary.

To Assemble
Divide the vegetable mixture evenly among six dinner plates. Top with a portion of black cod and garnish with a slice of pancetta. Ladle a little sauce over each plate.

Tip
You can ask your fishmonger to scale the black cod before you buy it or you can do it yourself: To scale the fish, place a knife at a 90-degree angle to the skin and gently scrape the skin with the blade, working from the tail toward the head. Use light, short, controlled movements. Use your bare hands to check for any remaining scales and gently scrape them away with the edge of your knife. Flip the fillet over and remove the pin bones in the flesh with tweezers or needle-nose pliers. Rinse the fillet under cold water and pat dry with a paper towel.

Pangaea

is a large restaurant that can seat over 120 patrons at once, but it's a slightly slower-paced establishment with a more food-focused clientele than the one I left to open it. So when I created the first menu for Pangaea back in 1996, I was excited to be able to reinvent a French classic as a modern, lighter version.

Ballotine is a French preparation that I think deserves reviving. The word describes a technique for boning, stuffing, and rolling meat into a log shape before braising or roasting it. My modernized, lighter version contains a lot of vegetables, which leads many people to say that it reminds them of sushi. Ballotine of rabbit has been on the spring Pangaea menu almost since the beginning. This fine-textured, snow-white meat is supremely tender. Prepare it for a special occasion when you really want to make an impression!

For 6 servings

Rabbit
2 dressed rabbits, each about 2 lbs (1 kg)
Salt and freshly ground pepper to taste
1 tbsp (15 mL) canola oil

Stuffing
4 cups (1 L) lightly packed stemmed baby
    spinach leaves
1 large carrot
2 stalks celery
1 leek, halved and washed
2 pig's cauls, soaked (optional)
3/4 tsp (4 mL) salt or to taste
3/4 tsp (4 mL) freshly ground black pepper
    or to taste

Mushroom Tian
1 tbsp (15 mL) canola oil
2 cups (500 mL) fresh cremini mushrooms,
    cleaned and quartered
2 tbsp (30 mL) white wine
1/3 cup (75 mL) rabbit reduction or chicken
    reduction (see pages 209–10)
2 cups (500 mL) lightly packed
    baby spinach leaves
1/2 cup (125 mL) finely diced, peeled,
    seeded tomato
1 tsp (5 mL) finely chopped fresh sage
1 tbsp (15 mL) finely chopped fresh parsley
Salt and freshly ground black pepper
6 sprigs micro-greens or fresh herbs

Note

To find caul fat, call ahead to the butcher shop and ask them to get some in for you, since this is what will baste the ballotine while it cooks. When you get it home, place the caul fat in warm salted water and gently and carefully pull apart the lacy folds of the membrane. You can make this recipe without the caul fat and it will still be very delicious; however, it may not have the same even outside colouring or hold together as well when you serve it.

Rabbit

Place the rabbit on its back and remove the organs (kidney, liver, and heart) and any cavity fat. Use a cleaver to remove the hind legs and the head (reserve for another use, such as making rabbit jus).

Beginning at the hind end, using the length of the knife, run the blade under each point of the spine, cutting away as little meat as possible. Continue until you reach the back of the rabbit's rib cage and the final point at the spine (lumbar vertebrae). Repeat on the other side, leaving the final point of the spine attached to the muscles. From the neck of the rabbit, run the tip of the knife between the ribs and the meat and work your way down the rib cage toward the spine. Scrape the meat away from the edge of the spine, working your way toward the hind end, lifting the spine free as you go. Remove the front legs (reserve for another use); remove any small or splintered small bones. Repeat with second rabbit.

Turn rabbits so that one long side is facing you. Cut the tenderloins in half lengthwise to even out the thickness of the rabbit across the back of the rib-cage area, then unfold to resemble a book that lies flat (butterfly). Season with salt and pepper.

Stuffing

Blanch the spinach in boiling salted water. Drain, refresh in an ice bath, and pat dry. Julienne the carrot, celery, and leek. Blanch each vegetable separately in boiling salted water. Drain, refresh, pat dry, and reserve.

Ballotines

Layer an equal portion of spinach evenly over the inside of each of the seasoned rabbits, leaving a border of meat exposed along the top edges. Side by side, make rows of each vegetable down the centre of each piece of meat where the spines were removed. Beginning at the edges closest to you, roll the rabbits into neat cylinders that encase the vegetables.

Drain the caul fat (if using), rinse, and squeeze out excess moisture. Spread the fat out, pat dry, and stretch gently. Trim 2 pieces of caul fat so that each is the same size or slightly bigger than the rolled pieces of rabbit.

Place one rolled rabbit, seam-side down, at the bottom edge of a piece of the caul fat. Roll rabbit tightly to encase in the caul fat. Truss with butcher's string, leaving enough slack in the twine to allow for expansion as the meat cooks. Repeat with second rabbit. (Ballotines can be made to this point, wrapped tightly in plastic wrap, and refrigerated for up to 1 day.)

To cook the ballotines, preheat the oven to 350°F (180°C). Pat the exterior of the ballotines dry and season with additional salt and pepper. Pour the oil into a large cast-iron pan set over medium-high heat and sear the ballotines until lightly browned on all sides. Place on a rimmed baking tray and transfer to preheated oven; roast for 20 minutes, turning

once. Remove from oven and allow to rest for 7 to 10 minutes before slicing.

Mushrooms
Heat the oil in a large skillet set over medium-high heat. When the oil begins to smoke, add the mushrooms and sauté for 5 to 6 minutes or until soft and golden brown. Add the white wine and rabbit jus; bring to a simmer. Add the spinach, tomato, sage, and parsley. Season to taste with salt and pepper.

To Assemble
Place a 3-inch (7.5 cm) cookie cutter, ring, or mould, in the centre of six serving plates. Place one-sixth of mushrooms into this mould, pressing to make a tight arrangement. Slice each ballotine into 9 equal slices and arrange slices around each mushroom tian. Garnish the top of each tian with a bouquet of micro-greens.

Tip
Ask the butcher to bone the rabbit for you if you don't want to fuss with this step yourself. Boning a rabbit is like boning two separate animals. Its skeletal structure changes at the midway point of the spine. The spine at the back half of the rabbit has five points, like a star, and the knife must navigate around each of these points with even strokes, cutting away as little meat as possible. The front rib-cage section is more straightforward, except that along the edge of the back there is one row of pin bones (thoracic vertebrae) to watch out for. You want to separate the meat from the skeleton in one complete piece, working on each side separately.

Ballotine of Rabbit
Stuffed with Julienne of Carrot,
Celery, and Leeks

Wild Mushroom Risotto

Wild mushroom risotto

Wild mushroom risotto is one of the dishes for which I'm best known, even though Pangaea is not an Italian restaurant. Reviewers wax poetic about it, and my wife even credits this dish with getting her through labour!

I use whatever wild mushrooms are most abundantly available, and truthfully, this dish is on the menu almost all year round as a result. In spring it often features morels and chanterelles, but when wild foraged mushrooms aren't available, I use locally cultivated mushrooms such as shiitake and cremini to make it, too.

For 4 servings

Mushrooms
1 tbsp (15 mL) butter
1 tbsp (15 mL) olive oil
2 cups (500 mL) assorted mushrooms, such as morels, chanterelles, yellowfoots, black trumpets
2 tsp (10 mL) minced shallot
1/2 tsp (2 mL) minced garlic
2 tbsp (30 mL) white wine
1 tsp (5 mL) freshly squeezed lemon juice
1 tsp (5 mL) finely chopped fresh sage
Salt and freshly ground black pepper

Risotto
3 tbsp (45 mL) butter, divided
2 tbsp (30 mL) olive oil
1/2 cup (125 mL) finely diced Spanish onion
2 cups (500 mL) Superfino Arborio or Carnaroli rice
1 bay leaf
1 tbsp (15 mL) minced garlic
1 cup (250 mL) white wine
5 cups (1.25 L) double-strength chicken stock (see page 208), heated
1 1/2 cups (375 mL) grated Parmigiano-Reggiano cheese
1 tsp (5 mL) balsamic vinegar
1 tsp (5 mL) truffle oil (optional)

Mushrooms
In a large skillet set over medium-high heat, heat the butter and oil. When the butter begins to foam, add the mushrooms and sauté. Cook for 3 to 5 minutes or until the mushrooms are well browned. Add the shallots and garlic. Sauté for 30 seconds and stir in white wine and lemon juice. Remove from heat and stir in sage; season to taste with salt and pepper and keep warm.

Risotto
In a large, heavy-bottomed saucepan set over medium-high heat, melt 1 tbsp (15 mL) of the butter with the oil. Once the butter begins to foam, add the onion and sauté for 2 to 3 minutes or until soft and translucent. Add the rice and sauté, stirring and scraping the bottom of the saucepan continuously with a wooden spoon, until the rice begins to toast and the edges become slightly translucent.

Stir in the bay leaf, garlic, and white wine and wait for the first bubbles to appear around the edge of the pan. Begin adding the stock, 1 cup (250 mL) at a time. Between each addition of stock, stir the mixture with the wooden spoon for 2 to 4 minutes or until the liquid is almost completely absorbed. Repeat this step until all but the last 1 cup (250 mL) of stock is used (this process should take approximately 20 to 25 minutes). Add the remaining stock and, using the wooden spoon, stir the risotto vigorously during the last minute of cooking.

To Assemble
Fold the mushrooms into the risotto. Gently stir in the remaining butter, the Parmesan, and balsamic vinegar. Divide the risotto evenly among four heated dishes, drizzle with truffle oil (if using), and serve immediately.

Lamb Rack
with Sunflower Crust, Fiddleheads,
and Cattail Hearts

Succulent, tender, evenly cooked meat is the mouth-watering result of a signature roasting technique I've developed and use often at Pangaea. Here I use this method to bring succulent Ontario lamb to optimum doneness (what classically trained chefs call *à point*). By coaxing the heat through the rack gently, this technique guarantees that the meat turns a uniform pink from edge to centre.

As a perfect and simple springtime accompaniment, we serve roasted lamb with cattail hearts and ostrich fern fiddleheads, two wild springtime forest vegetables. Jonathan Forbes finds these foods for us. In late spring, he and his crew visit the marshes, wetlands, and shallow lakes in the Laurentian Mountains to find cattail hearts, which are similar to hearts of palm but more tender and flavourful. Jonathan and his team snap the stalks from near the roots and then trim each cattail heart like a leek.

For 6 servings

Vegetables

2 cups (500 mL) water
1 tbsp (15 mL) granulated sugar
1 tbsp (15 mL) freshly squeezed lemon juice
1/2 tsp (2 mL) kosher salt
2 cups (500 mL) 1 1/2-inch (4 cm) pieces cattail hearts
2 cups (500 mL) fiddleheads
2 tbsp (30 mL) unsalted butter
1/3 cup (75 mL) lightly packed fresh Italian parsley leaves
Salt and freshly ground black pepper

Lamb

3 whole lamb racks, frenched
1 tsp (5 mL) salt
1 tsp (5 mL) freshly ground pepper
3 tbsp (45 mL) liquid honey
3 tbsp (45 mL) Dijon mustard
1/4 tsp (1 mL) ground cloves
1 tsp (5 mL) finely chopped fresh rosemary leaves
1 tsp (5 mL) coarsely crushed black peppercorns
Pinch freshly grated nutmeg
1 tsp (5 mL) minced garlic
1 tsp (5 mL) minced jalapeño pepper
2 tbsp (30 mL) vegetable oil
3/4 cup (175 mL) sunflower seeds

Vegetables

In a saucepan set over medium-high heat, combine the water with the sugar, lemon juice, and salt. Add the cattail hearts and bring to a boil. Reduce heat to a simmer, cover, and cook for 8 to 10 minutes. Remove from heat and let stand for 10 minutes. Transfer cattail hearts to a tray; spread evenly and cool to room temperature. Refrigerate until needed. Discard cooking liquid.

Heat a fresh saucepan filled with salted water to a boil. Wash the fiddleheads thoroughly in several changes of cold water. Drain well and trim the bases. Plunge the fiddleheads into the boiling water and cook for 5 minutes. Transfer the fiddleheads to a bowl filled with ice water and let stand until completely chilled. Drain well and refrigerate until needed.

Lamb

Preheat oven to 400°F (200°C). Scrape the bones of the lamb racks so they are smooth and clean. Pat lamb dry with a paper towel and season the outside with salt and pepper.

In a small metal bowl, combine the honey, Dijon mustard, cloves, rosemary, crushed peppercorns, nutmeg, garlic, and jalapeño; mix well.

Heat the oil in a skillet set over high heat; add the oil and heat until smoking. Add the lamb and sear evenly on both sides and edges until golden brown, about 2 minutes. Transfer to a rimmed baking sheet and rest for 10 minutes.

Roast the lamb in the preheated oven for 15 minutes, turning once. Remove and let rest for 5 minutes.

Pat the outside of the lamb dry. Coat the meaty side of each rack evenly with the honey-mustard mixture and press the sunflower seeds into the honey-mustard to form a crust. Return the lamb to the oven and roast for an additional 8 minutes for rare (115°F/46°C) or 12 minutes for medium-rare (120°F/49°C). Remove from oven and rest for at least 10 minutes before slicing between the bones into chops.

To Serve

While the lamb rests, heat the vegetables: Place a small skillet over medium heat; add butter. When butter begins to foam, add fiddleheads and toss well. Add cattail hearts; toss gently and season to taste. When vegetables are hot to the touch, toss in parsley leaves and transfer to a serving dish.

On a cutting board, hold the lamb rack with the bones pointing up and the curve of the loin facing you. Place the blade of the knife between the bones and slice into even-sized chops. Place the lamb chops on a serving tray.

I discovered

I discovered — quite by accident — that this is the perfect recipe for people who always overcook their meat. Here's what happened. One day a customer ordered this entrée and requested that it be cooked well done. I cooked it for the required time and did a quick check of the vitals: a touch for firmness, a visual for required shrinkage, internal temperature check — it all looked good. "Setup on table 41!" I declared, and the kitchen prepared the rest of the food for the table.

One last cut was all that was left to complete the plate. "What? Why is this meat still pink inside?" I asked myself after I had cut into it. "We have to go around!" I ordered (that's what we say when the conditions to serve a table are not right.) "The customer wants it dead!" the waiter exclaimed, uninvited, when he saw the state of the meat.

So we started again. "Setup 41!" was called a second time, and yet again the meat was pink! And then it hit me. The meat was well done, but the sodium nitrate from the Swiss chard had preserved the colour. This crude salt in leafy greens has been used historically as a natural preservative for meat, as in the more commonly known saltpetre. So the meat was technically well done, but the colour was the pretty pink of medium and would not darken further.

We explained the science of the matter to our customer, but he wasn't convinced that we could cook a piece of meat to well done to save our lives.

For 6 servings

Red Wine Shallot Sauce
1 tbsp (15 mL) unsalted butter
2 tbsp (30 mL) chopped shallots
1/2 tsp (2 mL) coarsely ground black pepper or to taste
1 bay leaf
1/2 clove garlic, minced
1 cup (250 mL) red wine, such as Cabernet Sauvignon
5 cups (1.25 L) veal stock (see page 210)
1/4 tsp (1 mL) finely chopped fresh thyme leaves
Salt
1 tsp (5 mL) cold butter cubes

Potato Mousseline
2 large russet (or 3 Yukon Gold) potatoes
1 1/2 cups (375 mL) half-and-half (10%) cream
6 tbsp (90 mL) unsalted butter
3/4 tsp (4 mL) salt
Pinch freshly grated nutmeg

Beef Roulade
2.2 lbs (1 kg) centre-cut beef tenderloin roast (see note page 69)
1 bunch Swiss chard
1 tbsp (15 mL) butter
1 tbsp (15 mL) minced shallot
1 lb (500 g) fresh black trumpet mushrooms
1 tsp (5 mL) minced garlic
1 tbsp (15 mL) white wine
1/4 tsp (1 mL) freshly squeezed lemon juice
1/4 tsp (1 mL) minced jalapeño pepper
3/4 tsp (4 mL) salt, divided
3/4 tsp (4 mL) freshly cracked black pepper, divided
1/2 clove garlic, minced
1 tbsp (15 mL) canola oil

Red Wine Shallot Sauce

In a large saucepan set over medium-high heat, melt the butter until it begins to foam. Add the shallots, pepper, and bay leaf. Sauté for 1 minute or until the shallots are golden. Stir in the garlic and cook for 30 seconds.

Deglaze with the red wine and simmer for 20 minutes or until the liquid is reduced by about half. Add the veal stock; bring to a boil. Reduce heat to low and simmer, skimming off any foam that develops, for 2 hours or until the sauce is thick enough to coat the back of a spoon.

Strain through a fine sieve, pressing the solids down with the back of a ladle or a spoon to remove all the fluid. Stir the thyme into the sauce; taste and season with salt and additional pepper if necessary. (Sauce can be made to this point up to 3 days ahead and reheated just before use.) Makes 1/3 cup (75 L).

Potato Mousseline

Preheat the oven to 375°F (190°C). Place the potatoes on a tray and bake for 1 1/2 hours (70 minutes if using Yukon Golds). When the cooking time is almost up, combine the cream, butter, salt, and nutmeg in a small saucepan set over medium heat; bring just to a boil. Remove from heat and keep warm.

Cut the potatoes into thirds; remove and discard the peels. Pass through a ricer into a metal bowl. Alternatively, chop the potatoes into chunks and mash finely. Blend the cream mixture into the potatoes until light and fluffy; taste and adjust seasoning if necessary. Cover and keep warm.

Beef Roulade

Trim the beef, ensuring that all the silver skin and sinew (the translucent connective tissue that can tighten and make the meat seem tough if left on during cooking) is removed. Place the beef on a cutting board so that one of the short ends is closest to you. Using a sharp chef's knife, make a slit down the length of the roast about 1/2 inch (1 cm) from the cutting board. Holding the knife against the meat at this slit, place your free hand on top of the roast. Turning the meat very slowly, cut so that it unrolls into a rectangular piece that is 1/2 inch (1 cm) thick. Reserve in refrigerator.

Remove the stems and any tough ribs from the Swiss chard and wash the leaves thoroughly in two changes of water. In a large pot

Roulade of Beef Tenderloin with Swiss Chard, Black Trumpet Mushrooms, and Creamy Potato Mousseline

of boiling salted water, blanch the chard for 1 minute. Drain and transfer to an ice bath; chill for 2 minutes or until very soft but still intact. Remove, drain, and lightly squeeze out excess water. Pat the chard dry between layers of paper towel. Reserve in refrigerator.

In a skillet set over medium-high heat, melt the butter. When the butter begins to foam, add the shallots and sauté until translucent. Add the mushrooms; sauté for a minute and add the minced garlic. Cook for an additional minute. Add the white wine and lemon juice and simmer until pan is almost dry. Remove from heat and stir in jalapeño, salt, and cracked pepper. Cool to room temperature.

Season the cut side of the reserved beef with ¼ tsp (1 mL) each of the salt and cracked pepper. Spread the garlic over the cut side of

the meat. Drape an even layer of the Swiss chard over the meat, then a layer of black trumpet mushrooms. Roll the beef snugly and tie off with butcher's string.

Preheat oven to 375°F (190°C). In an oven-proof skillet set over medium-high, heat the oil. Season the outside of the roast evenly all over with the remaining salt and pepper. When the oil is hot, sear the outside of the beef until golden brown on all sides, about 5 minutes. Rest the meat at room temperature for 10 minutes.

Transfer the meat to the oven and roast on the middle rack for 30 minutes or until cooked to medium-rare (140°F/60°C). Remove from oven and allow roulade to rest for 10 minutes before cutting into 6 equal portions.

To Assemble

Reheat the sauce until hot; remove from heat and whisk in the bits of butter.

Divide the Potato Mousseline among six warmed plates, placing each portion in the middle. Slice the Beef Roulade into medallions and place on top of the potatoes. Spoon sauce around potato and serve at once.

Note

When you buy the meat for this recipe, explain to the butcher that it must be a piece cut from the centre section of the beef tenderloin. Pieces from the tail end will be too narrow to butterfly and pieces from the head end will feature three separate muscles that can be tied together to make steaks but can't be cut into one flat piece.

Our friends

Lynn and Joe Siegal of Hilite Fine Foods carry in most of the rhubarb that comes through the door at Pangaea. Often this rhubarb comes from Lennox Farm, in Dufferin County near Shelburne, Ontario. The farm is owned and operated by Bill French, a fifth-generation farmer whose main crops are rhubarb and peas. Although I haven't been there myself, my wife, Dana, has had a guided tour of the dark barns where Bill winters his rhubarb plants so they are mature enough to force late each winter.

For 6 servings

Puff Pastry

¾ cup (175 mL) all-purpose flour (approx.)
⅓ cup (75 mL) cake and pastry flour
¼ tsp (1 mL) salt
¾ cup (175 mL) cold butter, cubed
5 tbsp (75 mL) ice water

Pastry Cream

1 cup (250 mL) whole (homogenized) milk
¼ tsp (1 mL) grated orange zest
½ vanilla bean, scraped
⅓ cup (75 mL) granulated sugar
3 egg yolks
2 tbsp (30 mL) cornstarch, sifted

Baked Rhubarb

1 vanilla bean
2 cups (500 mL) granulated sugar
3 lbs (1.5 kg) rhubarb, ¾-inch (2 cm) thick

Rhubarb Sorbet

4 cups (1 L) reserved baked rhubarb
    and syrup (see above)
1 cup (250 mL) cold water

Candied Kumquats

12 kumquats
½ cup (125 mL) water
1¾ cups (425 mL) granulated sugar
1 tbsp (15 mL) freshly squeezed lemon juice

1½ cups (375 mL) chantilly cream
    (see page 213)
Crème Anglaise (see page 213)
Confectioners' (icing) sugar

The result of Bill's ingenious farming techniques is that we have fantastic-quality local rhubarb to cook with as early as February! Colen Quinn, our pastry chef, transforms these bubblegum-coloured stalks into a sophisticated dessert plate that contrasts creamy with crunchy and flaky, as well as sweet with tangy.

Puff Pastry

Combine the all-purpose flour, cake and pastry flour, and salt in the bowl of a stand mixer. Add the butter cubes and toss to coat. Using the paddle attachment, beat on low for 20 seconds or until about half the butter cubes have blended with flour to make a crumbly texture. Still beating on low, add the water and blend until a very ragged dough forms.

Turn out onto a piece of plastic wrap. Using the wrap as a guide, press the bits of dough together so that the butter and flour are evenly distributed and the dough makes a 6-inch (15 cm) square. Tightly wrap and refrigerate for 30 minutes or until firm.

Using the side of a rolling pin, pat the wrapped dough down to compress into a disk. Loosen the wrapping but leave the dough covered. Roll out the dough, pressing any loose edges into the dough as necessary, into an 11- by 7-inch (28 by 18 cm) rectangle. Use the plastic wrap to help fold in the dough from one narrow side. Lay the wrap back down on the counter and fold over the other end of dough like a letter being folded to go into an envelope. Rewrap dough in same plastic wrap. Chill for 30 minutes or until quite firm.

Repeat this step five more times.

After the last chilling time, place the cold dough on a clean work surface so that the edge of the top fold faces away from you. Roll in the direction of the fold, adding a little extra flour if necessary, to make an 11- by 15-inch (28 by 38 cm) rectangle. Transfer to a parchment-lined, rimmed baking sheet. Refrigerate for 30 minutes.

Preheat the oven to 400°F (200°C). Cover the pastry with another piece of parchment paper and another rimmed baking sheet. Bake for 25 minutes. Remove the top tray and layer of parchment paper. Bake for an additional 5 minutes or until a pale golden colour. Cool completely.

Using a serrated knife, trim any uneven edges so the puff pastry has straight sides. Slice lengthwise down the centre of the puff pastry and then crosswise six times to make 12 pieces. Set 6 pieces aside. Using a knife with small serrations, cut each of the remaining pieces in half to make two layers. (You should have 6 pieces of pastry of full thickness and 12 layers of pastry of half thickness.)

Pastry Cream

Place the milk in a saucepan. Add the orange zest and vanilla pod and scraped seeds; whisk in half of the sugar. Set over medium-high heat. Heat until bubbles begin to form around the edge of the pan and the milk just begins to bubble. Remove pan from heat.

Quickly beat the eggs with the remaining sugar and the cornstarch until very smooth. Whisk a little of the hot milk into the egg mixture until smooth. Using a rubber spatula, scrape the egg mixture into the saucepan.

Cook, whisking constantly, for 2 minutes or until the custard is smooth and very thick. Remove from the heat and discard vanilla pod. Transfer pastry cream to a mixing bowl and cover with plastic wrap touching the surface of the custard. Cool to room temperature. Chill until ready to use.

Rhubarb Mille Feuille with Rhubarb Sorbet, Candied Kumquats, and Crème Anglaise

Baked Rhubarb

Preheat the oven to 375°F (190°C). Halve the vanilla bean lengthwise and scrape the seeds off with the edge of a knife. In a 9- by 13-inch (23 by 33 cm) glass baking dish, combine the sugar and vanilla seeds and rub them together until evenly combined. Measure out half the sugar and place in another 9- by 13-inch (23 by 33 cm) glass baking dish. Add one half of the scraped vanilla pod to each dish.

Trim the rhubarb and cut into 2-inch (5 cm) lengths. Add half the rhubarb to each baking dish and toss to coat evenly. Bake in pre-heated oven for 20 minutes. Gently stir and bake for 5 minutes longer or until rhubarb is very soft but still holds its shape. Cool completely in baking dishes. Transfer 84 of the best-looking rhubarb pieces to a clean, dry container. Cover tightly and refrigerate for up to 2 days. Measure the remaining rhubarb and cooking juices and set aside 4 cups (1 L) to use in the sorbet. Discard vanilla beans.

Rhubarb Sorbet

Combine the measured rhubarb and syrup in a high-speed blender; add the water, and purée until very smooth. Chill completely. Transfer to a chilled ice cream maker and proceed according to manufacturer's instructions until mixture is thickened. Transfer to a tub that seals tightly and freeze until set enough to scoop.

Alternatively, transfer the cooled mixture to a shallow, non-reactive pan; place in freezer. Stir occasionally with whisk as crystals begin to form. Continue to freeze until the mixture is set and has formed a finely grainy texture.

Candied Kumquats

Trim and discard the ends from each kumquat. Slice into $1/4$-inch (1 mL) thick slices. Using a wooden skewer or the tip of a paring knife, poke the seeds out of each slice and discard. Reserve prepared slices.

Combine the water, sugar, and lemon juice in a saucepan set over medium-high heat. Cook, stirring, until the sugar is dissolved. Bring to a boil. Add the reserved fruit, stirring to coat and separate. Reduce heat to medium-low and simmer for 5 to 8 minutes or until kumquats are translucent in the centre. Cool completely in syrup. Transfer to a clean, dry, airtight container and refrigerate for up to 1 week. Drain off syrup before using.

To Assemble

Just before assembling the dessert, beat the pastry cream, using an electric mixer fitted with a whisk attachment from 1 to 2 minutes, until very smooth.

On a large rectangular serving plate, set one of the thinner pieces of puff pastry on the left-hand side so that the narrow end of the pastry is at a right angle to the long end of the plate. Drop 3 small spoonfuls of pastry cream over the pastry and smooth to cover evenly. Spread 7 slices of reserved rhubarb across the pastry cream to cover it completely. Using two table-spoons, make 2 quenelles of chantilly cream and centre one over the top half and one over the lower half of the bed of fruit. Top with a thicker piece of puff pastry. Repeat pastry cream, fruit, and chantilly cream layers. Dust a thinner piece of puff pastry with confectioners' sugar; place, sugar-side up, on top of stacked fruit, cream, and pastry. Place the crème anglaise in a squeeze bottle and drizzle around the mille feuille to form a frame.

In the centre of the serving plate, spoon a few Candied Kumquats. On the right-hand side of the plate, place a small scoop of rhubarb sorbet.

Repeat with remaining ingredients on five more plates.

Maple Pecan Tart
with Buttermilk Ice Cream,
Plum Compote,
and Candied Orange Zest

Maple syrup

is one of the wonders of spring in my part of the world. Each autumn, maple trees produce a supply of starch to sustain their roots over the long frozen winter. As the weather warms and spring causes the snow to melt, water enters the tree's roots and enzymes change this starch into "sugar water" that circulates through the tree, preparing it for the new growing season. The sap itself is thin, colourless, and not terribly sweet. In fact, the distinctive "maple" taste develops only after the sap is reduced to a wonderful, dark amber syrup. It takes 10 gallons (40 L) of sap to make 1 quart (1 L) of syrup, so every drop is precious and deserves to be showcased in a delicious recipe like this tart that takes inspiration from a Southern US classic but delivers a true Canadian maple flavour.

This might be my favourite dessert on the Pangaea menu. It's a study in contrasts: sweet, toasty nuts and pastry; tangy, fruity compote; creamy yet palate-cleansing buttermilk ice cream; and, last, candied orange that acts as a bridge to all these other flavours.

For 6 servings

Plum Compote
1¼ cups (300 mL) granulated sugar
4 firm black plums
½ vanilla bean, halved lengthwise and scraped
2 tbsp (30 mL) freshly squeezed lemon juice

Buttermilk Ice Cream
1 cup (250 mL) whipping (35%) cream
1¼ cups (300 mL) granulated sugar, divided
6 egg yolks
1 cup (250 mL) buttermilk

Candied Orange Zest
½ cup (125 mL) water
¾ cup (175 mL) granulated sugar, divided
1 navel orange

Pastry
½ cup (125 mL) chilled butter, cubed
⅓ cup (75 mL) granulated sugar
¼ tsp (1 mL) vanilla extract
1¼ cups (300 mL) all-purpose flour
Pinch salt

Filling
⅓ cup (75 mL) butter, melted
½ cup (125 mL) lightly packed dark brown sugar
½ cup (125 mL) best-quality maple syrup
1 tsp (5 mL) vanilla extract
Pinch salt
2 eggs, beaten
¾ cup (175 mL) coarsely chopped toasted pecans

Plum Compote
Preheat the oven to 350°F (180°C). Place the sugar in a 9- by 13-inch (23 by 33 cm) glass baking dish. Slice the plums in half; remove and discard the pits. Cut each plum into 8 wedges. Add the vanilla and lemon juice. Toss well and arrange fruit in a single layer. Bake the plums in preheated oven for 25 minutes or until sugar has formed a syrup and is bubbling around the edges of the pan, stirring twice during cooking. Spoon sauce over the plums and cool completely. Transfer to a clean, dry container; cover tightly and refrigerate for at least 8 hours or for up to 2 days.

Buttermilk Ice Cream
Combine the cream and ½ cup (125 mL) of the sugar in a saucepan. Bring the mixture to a boil. Remove from heat.

Whisk the eggs with the remaining sugar. Drizzle a little of the hot cream mixture into the egg mixture and whisk until smooth. Scrape the egg mixture into the saucepan and whisk to combine well. Place over medium heat and cook, whisking constantly, for 1 minute. Remove from heat and whisk in the buttermilk. Strain the mixture into a bowl and cool to room temperature. Chill completely in the refrigerator.

Transfer the chilled mixture to an ice cream machine and churn according to manufacturer's instructions. Transfer to a tub that seals tightly and freeze until set enough to scoop.

Candied Orange Zest
Combine the water and ½ cup (125 mL) of the sugar in a small saucepan. Stir to combine. Place over medium-high heat and bring to a boil. Meanwhile, using a vegetable peeler, peel the orange in thick strips from the stem to the base end. Lay each strip, pith-side up, on a cutting board. Using the blade of a chef's knife, scrape away the pith and discard. Cut into long, thin strips.

Place the orange strips in the water mixture and bring to a boil. Reduce the heat to medium-low and simmer for 15 minutes or until the orange strips are translucent.

Remove from the liquid using a slotted spoon and drain on parchment paper for 3 to 5 minutes or until tacky. Spread the remaining sugar out on a plate and dredge the orange zest in the sugar. Shake off excess sugar and store the sugar-coated orange strips in a single layer in an airtight container.

Pastry
In the bowl of an electric stand mixer fitted with a paddle attachment, beat the butter with the sugar and vanilla on medium-high until light and fluffy; scrape down the bowl. Add the flour and salt. Beat for 1 minute on low until ingredients are moistened and crumbly; scrape down the bowl once.

Transfer mixture to a clean work surface dusted lightly with flour; knead until mixture holds together to form a smooth dough. Form into a log and wrap tightly with plastic wrap. Chill for 2 hours or until firm.

Place six 3½-inch (9 cm) bottomless ring moulds on a parchment-lined rimmed baking sheet and chill for 20 minutes. Cut dough into 6 equal portions. Roll each portion of dough into a 4½-inch (11 cm) circle. Press dough into rings. (To repair any cracks that form, press dough together until set.) Trim the dough with a small, sharp knife so it's flush with the top of the ring. Place the tray in the refrigerator.

Filling

Meanwhile, whisk the butter with the brown sugar, maple syrup, vanilla, and salt until smooth. Whisk in the eggs until well combined. Cover and chill. (Mixture can be made up to 3 days ahead.)

Preheat the oven to 375°F (190°C). Divide the pecans evenly between the chilled tart shells. Stir the filling and pour an equal amount into each tart shell. Bake the tarts for 20 to 25 minutes or until the crust is golden and the filling is set; cool completely on a rack. Turn tarts over and gently push the tarts out of the rings.

To Assemble

Place a pecan tart in the middle of a large serving plate. Garnish with 3 plum wedges and spoon the sauce from the plums around the tarts. Place a small scoop of buttermilk ice cream on each plate and garnish with candied orange zest. Repeat for five more plates. Serve with additional compote on the side.

Sum

mer

Summer in Canada is a giddy time for chefs. Local abundance is all around, making it oh so easy to create fantastic vegetable-based recipes.

Cookstown Greens

Most of the vegetables we use at Pangaea in spring, summer, and autumn come from Cookstown Greens, an organic farm north of Toronto. David Cohlmeyer founded this company long before eating organic food was fashionable or the term was even understood by most people. I've been his customer for almost 20 years, but when Pangaea opened, we forged an even closer relationship, with David growing special items for me that I wanted to add to the Pangaea menu but couldn't find other places. In turn, he's introduced me to wonderful heritage varieties of common vegetables such as carrots and tomatoes and unusual ingredients such as crosnes and dahlia roots and Burbank huckleberries.

We so value our working relationship with David that a couple of years ago when he was preparing to go to Slow Food's Terre Madre Conference in Italy, we sponsored his trip so that we could help him accomplish his culinary goals.

While David has many other customers and we buy produce from other suppliers, too, I'm proud that we've become such close partners. In fact, we often join forces to promote ourselves as a team. For instance, for the last two years we've shared a space at the Picnic at the Brick Works, a fundraiser for Evergreen and Slow Food Toronto. And in autumn 2009, David and I cooked for His Majesty the Prince of Wales at a Brick Works event. In fact, we ended up having a conversation about organic agriculture with the prince that lasted several minutes!

Wild Flowers

While some chefs toss flowers around with abandon on dessert plates, I'm not a big fan of using them in the sweet kitchen. That said, I do love the peppery, slightly bitter accent that a few random marigold leaves add to the spring-mix blend I've been buying from Cookstown Greens for years. What is really fantastic about Cookstown is that they grow greens and flowers all year long. In the summer they are grown organically outdoors, while in the winter rows of these tender greens thrive in their unique greenhouses that use ground soil.

Adding flowers to your cooking may seem simple enough, but making appropriate flavour matches can be difficult since each flower, like each fruit or vegetable, has its own distinct flavour.

Because it's hard to wash flowers thoroughly without damaging their delicate petals, I use only organically grown flowers that have never been fertilized with chemicals or dusted with pesticides. I wash them carefully by immersing each blossom quickly in cold water, then I shake each bloom gently and lay it to drain on a clean kitchen towel.

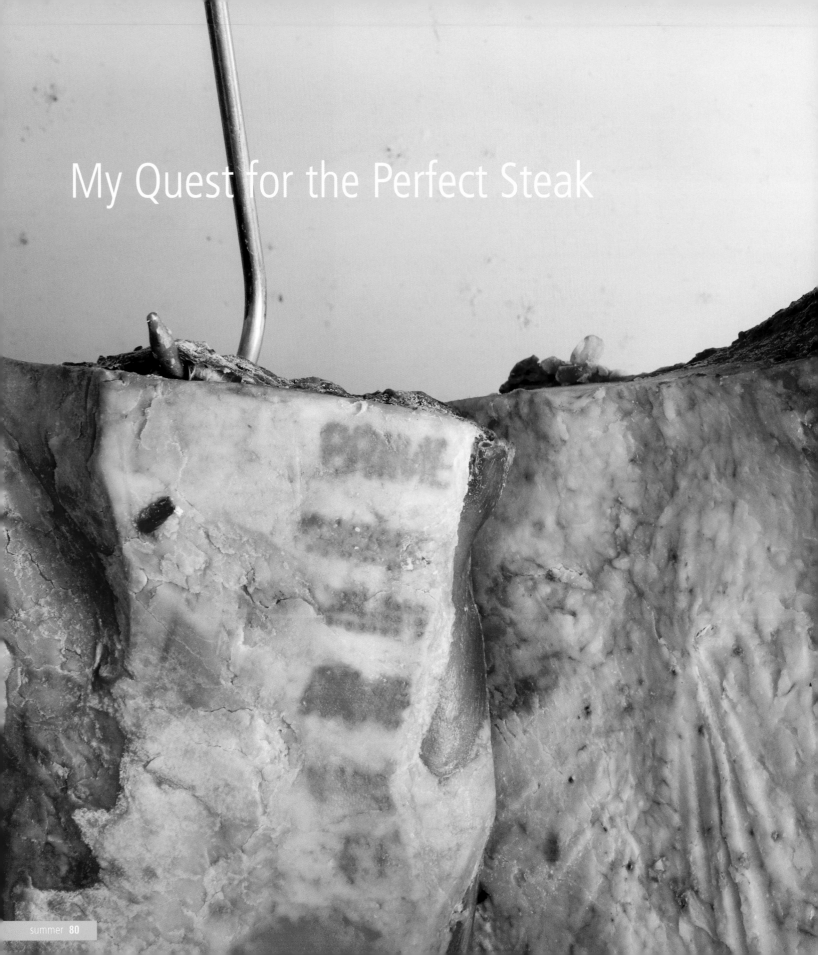

My Quest for the Perfect Steak

Fantastic

steaks should be easy to get in Canada — a country known for cattle ranching. But, while it's easy to get good steaks here, fantastic meat is not quite as easily attainable.

I like the taste of grain-finished steak; it needs to be juicy and flavourful, supremely tender, yet still toothsome. Such steaks are only available, in my opinion, from a butcher who dry-ages with care and uses his eyes and judgment — not just a calendar and a knife — to decide when a piece of meat is ready to be cooked.

To be honest, I'd love to age my own meat, but Pangaea is just too small; there's literally no extra room to install a locker for aging. Fortunately for me, I found Peter Bochna. He's a chef turned specialty grocer who really understands how to coax the best flavour out of a piece of beef. Peter buys his beef from Norwich Packers, a company that operates in Oxford County,

a couple of hours outside of Toronto. They comb the sales to buy the best Ontario steers available and then finish the meat on their dry lot. They deliver this premium-grade beef to Peter, and he assesses each piece and dry-ages it as necessary at his shop, Absolutely Fine Foods. Some pieces need to hang for six weeks, others for eight. It's about the process and not the time for Peter. Once he's satisfied with the texture and colour of the beef, he sends the whole strip loins to us to be portioned and grilled to our customer's preference.

Since we're known for selling such good ones, some of you may find it odd that there is no steak recipe in this book, but that's because good meat really doesn't need a recipe. All you

need to do is season it well and grill it on a hot grate until the meat reaches the desired internal temperature. And that's it. Hardly information that needs a full page to communicate!

Use my temperature guide and an instant-read thermometer to ensure that you cook your steak to match your preference. In all cases, preheat the grill until very hot. Wipe the grate of the grill with an oil-soaked rag and then reduce the heat to medium-high when you add the meat.

Temperature Guide

Steak Thickness	Rare 130°F (55°C)	Medium-Rare 145°F (63°C)	Medium 160°F (71°C)	Well-Done 170°C (77°C)
1½ inches (4 cm)	2 to 3 minutes per side	3 to 5 minutes per side	6 to 7 minutes per side	7 to 8 minutes per side
2 inches (5 cm)	4 to 5 minutes per side	6 to 7 minutes per side	7 to 8 minutes per side	9 to 11 minutes per side

Cheese

Being of Dutch extraction, I grew up eating cheese often. While my friends were toting lunchboxes loaded with white-bread sandwiches stuffed with processed-cheese slices, my mom was hand-slicing Gouda and Edam from wax-covered wheels for my lunches.

When I became a chef's apprentice, my love of cheese only grew. France and Italy were the gourmet sovereigns of cheese in those days. If the cheese wasn't imported, it wasn't good enough for most of the restaurants I worked at. Their bias seems laughable now, but it developed with good reason. Twenty years ago, most Canadian cheesemakers were looking for ways to become more automated and to emulate factory-made cheese methods. There really wasn't a lot of good-quality cheese in Canada, and finding the little bit that was produced was very difficult.

As the cheese-course trend emerged in prominent food cities such as New York and San Francisco, the perfume of their local artisan cheeses wafted over the border and encouraged Canadian cheese lovers to wonder if our milk might make good cheese, too.

Today, there's a plethora of great cheese being handmade right in the Ontario greenbelt. Upper Canada Cheese Company, Monforte, and Fifth Town Artisan Cheese are just a few of the cheesemakers we feature on our cheese board and in our recipes.

Likewise, we support exceptional cheeses from British Columbia and Quebec because knowledgeable cheese distributors like Cole Snell from Provincial Fine Foods make it easy for chefs to try the latest and greatest artisanal Canadian cheeses.

So while we still use kilos and kilos of Tuscan Parmesan each day, we're using more and more great cheeses that are made in Canada, too. In fact, we've started to make our own cheese, too.

Summer
recipes

Appetizers

Main Courses

Desserts

Triptych of Summer Soups
   Heirloom Tomato and Basil with Balsamic and Ginger Reduction
   Sugar Snap Pea with Buttermilk Crème Fraîche
   Corn and Fennel with Chanterelles

Good food
is something we take seriously at Pangaea; that said, we love life, and if we can make people smile, so much the better.

That's why our summer triptych is styled to look like a stoplight. The colours of these three soups are naturally suited to such a presentation, and it makes people stop and realize that a great meal is about to begin, too!

For 8 servings each of three soups

Heirloom Tomato and Basil Soup
2½ lbs (1.25 kg) heirloom tomatoes,
    about 7, all one colour
2 tsp (10 mL) canola oil
¼ cup (60 mL) diced onion
½ tsp (2 mL) chopped garlic
½ cup (125 mL) chicken stock
    (see page 208)
2 tsp (10 mL) peeled, minced fresh ginger
½ cup (125 mL) chopped fresh basil leaves
¾ tsp (4 mL) salt or to taste
1 tsp (5 mL) granulated sugar (optional)

Balsamic and Ginger Reduction
½ cup (125 mL) aged balsamic vinegar
1 tbsp (15 mL) peeled, minced fresh ginger
2 tsp (10 mL) brown sugar
8 basil bud tips

To Serve
Warm three small bowls per person. Spoon out even portions of the three soups and garnish with appropriate toppings.

Tips
If a soup thickens as it sits, adjust the texture by adding a little boiling water.

For vegetarian versions, substitute vegetable broth or water for the chicken stock.

Heirloom Tomato and Basil Soup
Preheat oven to 350°F (180°C). Cut an X in the skin of the tomatoes and blanch them by immersing in boiling water for 1 minute, then draining and refreshing under ice water. Drain well, peel, and chop.

In a large, non-reactive saucepan set over medium heat, heat the oil; add the onions and sauté until tender. Add the garlic and sauté until it just begins to colour. Add the tomatoes, stock, and ginger; bring to boil. Reduce heat and simmer for 10 minutes. Remove from heat and stir in basil and salt. Purée in a high-speed blender until smooth. Pass the mixture through a medium strainer; taste and add up to 1 tsp (5 mL) of sugar if the soup is too acidic. Adjust the seasoning if necessary, too.

Balsamic and Ginger Reduction
In a small, non-reactive saucepan set over medium-low heat, combine the balsamic vinegar, ginger, and brown sugar; bring to a boil. Reduce heat and simmer until syrupy, about 11 minutes. Strain through a fine strainer. Drizzle over tomato soup and garnish with a basil bud tip before serving.

Sugar Snap Pea Soup
1 tbsp (15 mL) butter
½ cup (125 mL) chopped leeks
¼ cup (60 mL) chopped celery
3 cups (750 mL) stringed, chopped sugar
    snap peas, divided
½ tsp (2 mL) salt or to taste
2½ cups (625 mL) chicken stock
    (see page 208)

Buttermilk Crème Fraîche
½ cup (125 mL) whipping (35%) cream
1 tbsp (15 mL) buttermilk
1 tsp (5 mL) finely chopped fresh mint

Sugar Snap Pea Soup
In a large saucepan set over medium heat, heat the butter until it foams. Add the leeks and celery; sauté until tender. Add 2 cups (500 mL) of the sugar snap peas, the salt, and stock. Bring to a boil; reduce heat and simmer for 5 minutes. Add remaining 1 cup (250 mL) of peas and bring just to a boil. Immediately remove from heat; purée in a high-speed blender. Pass the mixture through a medium strainer. Taste and adjust seasoning, if necessary.

Buttermilk Crème Fraîche
In a small saucepan set over low heat, warm the whipping cream until it registers 105°F (40°C) on an instant-read thermometer. Remove from heat and transfer to a heatproof glass jar. Stir in the buttermilk. Cover the jar with cheesecloth and let stand at room temperature for 24 to 36 hours. Stir the mixture well and refrigerate.

Just before serving, fold in the mint. Garnish each bowl of pea soup with a dollop of crème fraîche. Reserve any leftover crème fraîche for another use.

Corn and Fennel Soup
1 tbsp (15 mL) butter
1/4 cup (60 mL) chopped onion
2 cups (500 mL) corn kernels, about 3 cobs
1/2 cup (125 mL) diced fennel bulb
1 tsp (5 mL) chopped garlic
2 cups (500 mL) chicken stock
   (see page 208), approx.
1/2 tsp (2 mL) salt or to taste

Chanterelles
2 tsp (10 mL) unsalted butter
1 tsp (5 mL) minced shallots
1/4 cup (60 mL) small chanterelle mushrooms
1/4 tsp (1 mL) minced garlic
1/4 cup (60 mL) white wine
Freshly squeezed lemon juice
Salt and freshly ground black pepper

Corn and Fennel Soup
In a large saucepan set over medium heat, heat the butter until it foams; add the onions and sauté until tender. Add the corn, fennel, and garlic and cook for 10 minutes or until softened. Add the chicken stock and bring to a boil; reduce temperature to a simmer; cook for 20 minutes. Season with salt.

In a high-speed blender, purée the soup in batches; adjust with a little hot chicken stock to thin the consistency if necessary. Pass the mixture through a medium strainer; taste and adjust seasoning, if necessary.

Chanterelles
In a large skillet set over medium heat, heat the butter until it foams; add the shallots and sauté until tender. Add the chanterelles and sauté for 2 to 3 minutes or until tender. Add the minced garlic and deglaze with white wine. Simmer to reduce the wine by two-thirds and add a few drops of lemon juice. Taste and season with salt and pepper if necessary. Keep warm.

Stews

that simmer over the course of 12 hours create delicious results. (Chances are that many of you reading this book own slow cookers and know exactly what I mean.) Well, what if you took two weeks to make fish — that would make it really delicious, right?

Seriously, this recipe could easily be called a project, since making the tuna gravlax requires time and patience. The good news is that it's easy work and results in an intense, satisfying cured fish that is the texture of prosciutto. (If you've ever had bottarga, the Sardinian pressed, cured fish roe, you'll have a sense of what to expect from this preparation.) When the tuna gravlax is complete, you'll have more fish than you need to serve this dish once; however, I'm sure you'll find other uses for it, since it can add zip and flavour to salads, dips, pasta, and even pizza the same way as other cured meats.

For 10 servings

Tuna
2 lbs (1 kg) centre-cut bigeye (ahi) or tuna, about 3 inches (7.5 cm) square
3 cups (750 mL) coarse sea salt
3 cups (750 mL) Demerara sugar
3/4 cup (175 mL) freshly ground black pepper
1/4 cup (60 mL) extra virgin olive oil

Salad Dressing
2 tbsp (30 mL) piment d'espelette (see note, this page) or Spanish paprika
1 tbsp (15 mL) sherry vinegar
1 cup (250 mL) grapeseed oil

Toasted Almonds
1/4 cup (60 mL) whole natural almonds

Salad
2 cups (500 mL) baby salad greens
1/4 cup (60 mL) pitted green olives
2 cups (500 mL) halved cherry tomatoes

At Pangaea, we buy only pole-caught tuna. It's much more expensive than other tuna, but it's endorsed by Ocean Wise and other endangered fish advocates because there's no problem with bycatch. When tuna are caught with nets, for instance, it's not unusual for dolphins and other fish to be trapped and harmed as well.

Tuna
In a bowl, combine the salt, sugar, and pepper. Toss to combine evenly. Spread a 1/2-inch (1 cm) depth of this mixture in the bottom of a non-reactive pan large enough to hold the tuna. Pat the tuna dry with a paper towel and place in the pan. Completely cover the fish with the remaining salt mixture (if the fish isn't completely covered, make more of the mixture and add it over top). Cover the pan tightly with plastic wrap and refrigerate for 24 hours. Check periodically to ensure that the tuna is still well covered by the salt mixture and to drain off any liquid that accumulates.

The next day, rinse away the salt mixture and pat the tuna dry with a paper towel. Lay a piece of cheesecloth about twice as large as the tuna on a clean work surface. Place the tuna at one end and roll in the cheesecloth until fully encased. Fold in the ends and roll until the cheesecloth snugly bundles the fish. Truss closed with butcher's twine, leaving a long end you can knot. Hang the tuna from one of the racks in the refrigerator for at least 10 or for as long as 15 days.

Salad Dressing
Combine the piment d'espelette, vinegar, and oil in a blender. Blend until well combined; transfer to a clean container. Cover and infuse overnight before use.

Toasted Almonds
Preheat the oven to 325°F (160°C). Spread the almonds evenly on a baking sheet and roast for 10 minutes or until brown and fragrant. Remove from the oven and transfer to a cool plate. Cool to room temperature. Using the side of a chef's knife, gently crack the almonds into smaller pieces.

To Assemble
Unwrap the tuna and slice very thinly. On 10 rectangular plates, overlap 4 slices of tuna at each end. In a small bowl, toss the greens with just enough of the dressing to lightly coat the leaves. Place a small mound of salad in the middle of each plate. Toss the almonds, olives, and cherry tomatoes with a little more of the dressing; scatter over the greens. Drizzle the tuna with extra virgin olive oil and serve.

Tip
Any leftover tuna can be stored for up to 1 month. Wrap leftover fish in fresh cheesecloth and place in a plastic container with a tight lid. Refrigerate.

Note
Piment d'espelette is a mild French spice similar to paprika.

Tuna Gravlax
with Almonds and Olives

Seared Scallop
on Sweet Pea Purée with
Braised Pork Belly

One benefit of buying a **whole pig** is that you have lots of different pork parts to use, which means you can't get in a rut and do the same thing over and over again. You simply have to find ways to use each bit if you want to realize the best food cost.

Pork belly is the cut of meat used to make bacon, and in this recipe it's braised fresh instead of being smoked and thinly sliced.

We've been using untreated diver scallops at Pangaea for years. I love them and was thrilled to be able to go out harvesting scallops myself when I was in Newfoundland a couple of years ago (see pictures on page 42). Fortunately, I'm an advanced scuba diver and I own my own dry suit, because the water was only 1°C or 2°C (32°F to 34°F). We took the scallops we caught back to the diver's lodge, and I made a big skillet of pan-fried scallops for everyone staying there. It was a far simpler preparation than the appetizer here but still one of the best meals I've ever eaten.

For 6 appetizer or 2 entrée servings

Scallops

6 large (U-10, or under 10 per lb)
   diver-caught scallops
2 tbsp (30 mL) vegetable oil
Sea salt

Pork Belly

1 lb (500 g) pork belly
1 cup (250 mL) red wine
2 cups (500 mL) veal stock (see page 210)

Orange Shallot Sauce

1 tsp (5 mL) butter
1 tsp (5 mL) minced shallots
1/2 tsp (2 mL) minced garlic
1/4 tsp (1 mL) coarsely ground black pepper
1/3 cup (75 mL) red wine
1 tsp (5 mL) orange zest
1/4 tsp (1 mL) chopped fresh sage

Green Pea Purée

1 tbsp (15 mL) butter
1/4 cup (60 mL) chopped onion
1/2 tsp (2 mL) chopped garlic
1/4 cup (60 mL) white wine
1 cup (250 mL) shelled fresh green peas
3/4 tsp (4 mL) salt
1/2 cup (125 mL) water

Garnish

Chervil, parsley, or baby lettuce leaves

Scallops

If using fresh scallops in their shells, clean the scallops by opening the shells with a clam knife or another blunt knife with a broad, semi-flexible blade; separate the meaty part of the scallop from the sinews, corals, and membrane. Remove the knob-shaped muscle on the side of meaty portion. (If using shelled scallops, remove the knob-shaped muscle on the side.) Rinse cleaned scallops under cold water and pat dry with paper towels. Refrigerate until ready to cook.

Pork Belly

Peel away and discard the skin from the pork belly and cut the meat into 2-inch (5 cm) cubes. Heat a small skillet over medium-high heat and sear the pork belly on all sides until golden. Deglaze the pan with red wine and then add enough veal stock to completely cover the pork belly cubes. Once the stock comes to a boil, reduce the heat and simmer for 30 minutes or until the liquid is reduced and thickened and the meat is well glazed. During cooking, skim off any foam that develops on the top and turn the pork occasionally.

Remove the pork from the sauce and set aside. Strain the sauce and keep warm.

Orange Shallot Sauce

In a saucepan set over medium heat, melt the butter and sauté the shallots, garlic, and cracked pepper; cook until the garlic begins to colour very slightly. Deglaze with red wine; reduce the heat and simmer until the liquid is almost completely reduced. Whisk in the orange zest, sage, and the reserved pork belly reduction. Simmer gently for 5 minutes or until the sauce is thick enough to coat the back of a spoon. Skim away all the fat that rises to the top as the mixture simmers.

Green Pea Purée

In another small saucepan set over medium heat, melt the butter and sauté the onion for 2 minutes or until slightly softened. Add the garlic and deglaze with white wine. Reduce the heat to medium-low and simmer until the wine is reduced to half its original volume. Add the peas and salt; cover and cook for 5 minutes. Remove from heat.

Place the pea mixture and water in a food processor and purée until smooth. Strain into a small bowl through a medium sieve. Keep warm. (Mixture can be made up to 1 day ahead if covered tightly and refrigerated when cool.)

To Assemble

Heat a large heavy skillet over medium-high heat; add the 2 tbsp (30 mL) oil and heat well. Add the dry scallops to the hot oil and cook on both sides until golden brown. Once the scallops are coloured, season both sides with sea salt.

Spoon a little Orange Shallot Sauce into the centre of six serving plates. Place a dollop of the pea purée in the centre of the sauce, top with a seared scallop, and garnish with a portion of pork belly and a sprig of chervil, parsley, or baby lettuce.

Sausages

are being made by many young chefs these days, and I'm glad to see it. It's been one of my pleasures for almost two decades. I first made sausage at Pronto Ristorante in Toronto, and I still recall how surprised I was by how easy it is to do. Truthfully, if you have a hand-held meat grinder or a stand mixer with a grinder attachment, making fresh sausage is only slightly more complex than making a hamburger.

I used to be a big fan of Australian lamb, but in the last few years, Ontario lamb has become so much more consistent that it's now the only choice for me. Regrettably, a lot of other people have been turned on to Ontario lamb and suppliers literally can't keep up with demand! In fact, the Ontario Sheep Marketing Agency estimates that our province can satisfy only about 50% of the public's demand. Talk about a local food success story!

For 6 servings

Lamb Sausage
1 lb (500 g) boneless leg of lamb
1 egg, beaten
1/2 tsp (2 mL) minced garlic
1 tsp (5 mL) chopped fresh rosemary leaves
2 tsp (10 mL) chopped fresh parsley leaves
1 tsp (5 mL) chopped jalapeño pepper
1/2 tsp (2 mL) very coarsely ground black
    pepper
1 1/2 tsp (7 mL) Dijon mustard
1 1/2 tsp (7 mL) salt
1 tbsp (15 mL) olive oil
1 piece natural lamb casing

Balsamic Reduction
1/2 cup (125 mL) aged balsamic vinegar
1 tsp (5 mL) orange zest
1/2 clove garlic, not chopped
2 tsp (10 mL) brown sugar

Summer Vegetable Ratatouille
1 red bell pepper
1 Japanese eggplant
3 tbsp (45 mL) olive oil, divided
1 tsp (5 mL) salt
2 zucchini
3 tomatoes, about 12 oz (340 g) total
1/2 cup (125 mL) pitted Gaeta or other
    black olives
5 fresh basil leaves
1/2 tsp (2 mL) minced garlic
Salt and freshly ground black pepper
1 tbsp (15 mL) extra virgin olive oil (optional)
Fresh basil sprigs

Lamb Sausage

Chill a grinder and the meat in the refrigerator or freezer. Cut the cold raw lamb, including the fat, into bite-sized pieces. Using the coarse setting, feed the meat through the grinder into a large mixing bowl.

Add the egg, garlic, rosemary, parsley, jalapeño, pepper, mustard, and salt. Gently blend the ingredients thoroughly. Form a small test patty using 1 tbsp (15 mL) of the mixture and cook it in a skillet. Taste to check the seasonings; adjust if necessary.

Place the lamb mixture into the piston of a hand-cranked sausage-stuffing machine or attachment on a stand mixer. Pour the olive oil into the lamb casing and fit the casing onto the machine's funnel. Slowly force the sausage mixture into the casing, making sure that you don't overfill (the casing should be slack enough to twist easily to form links).

Pinch the stuffed lamb into sausages of approximately 5-inch (13 cm) lengths and twist to form links, twisting each link in the opposite direction from the last spin. Repeat until the entire length of stuffed casing has been made into links. Use kitchen scissors to cut the links apart.

Balsamic Reduction

In a small, non-reactive saucepan set over medium-low heat, combine the balsamic vinegar, orange zest, garlic, and brown sugar; bring to a boil. Reduce heat and simmer until syrupy, about 11 minutes. Strain through a fine strainer into a small glass jar.

Summer Vegetable Ratatouille

Roast the red pepper over an open flame or under the broiler to char the skin. Turn the pepper frequently to char evenly. Plunge the blackened pepper into ice water until completely cool. Peel away and discard the charred skin, then rinse the pepper and pat dry. Cut in half and remove the stem ball and seeds. Remove and discard the ribs. Dice the cleaned pepper. Reserve.

Slice the eggplant into 1/2-inch (1 cm) slices. Toss with 1 tsp (5 mL) of the olive oil to coat; sprinkle with salt. Remove the stem and slice the zucchini lengthwise into 1/4-inch (6 mm) strips. Toss with another 1 tsp (5 mL) of the olive oil. Grill both vegetables over medium heat or roast in a preheated 350°F (180°C) oven until soft. Cool completely and dice the eggplant and zucchini the same size as peppers. Reserve.

Meanwhile, score an X in the bottom of each tomato using a sharp paring knife. Blanch tomatoes in boiling water for 30 seconds. Drain well and plunge into ice water. Drain and pat dry. Peel, seed, and dice the tomatoes to the same size as the other vegetables (you should have about 1/2 cup/ 125 mL). Toss tomatoes with the remaining olive oil and a pinch of salt.

Combine the vegetables.

Finely dice the olives. Chop the basil coarsely. Combine with the minced garlic and diced vegetables. Season with salt and pepper to taste. Drizzle with extra virgin olive oil (if using). Do not refrigerate.

Lamb Sausage with Ratatouille of Summer Vegetables and Balsamic Reduction

To Assemble

Preheat the grill to medium high. Grease the grate. Grill the sausages for 5 minutes, turning often, or until medium-rare. Using two large kitchen spoons, form the ratatouille into 6 large quenelles by scooping the mixture from spoon to spoon until it resembles an egg with flat sides. Place a quenelle off-centre on a serving plate (you'll need six). Add 2 sausages, drizzle with a portion of balsamic reduction, and garnish with basil sprigs.

Tips

This sausage recipe doubles easily. Extra sausages can be flash frozen and then tightly wrapped and frozen for up to 1 month.

If you don't have a grill
- Sauté the eggplant in a non-stick skillet set over medium heat for 5 minutes per side. Transfer to a baking sheet and finish cooking in a preheated 350°F (180°C) oven for 20 minutes. Turn halfway through.
- Sauté the zucchini for 3 minutes per side in a non-stick skillet set over medium heat.
- Cook the sausages in a lightly greased non-stick skillet over medium-high heat. Cook for 5 to 7 minutes, turning often, until well browned on all sides and cooked to medium-rare.

Heirloom Tomato Salad

Heirloom

tomatoes need very little human intervention to be delicious. Cookstown Greens delivers cases of these multi-coloured fruits to our kitchen door all summer long. In fact, I'm not even going to give you a formal recipe for our very popular heirloom tomato salad since duplicating it is more about shopping than cooking.

Heirloom tomatoes have a great name; they sound like an inheritance from a wacky old auntie, and in a way they are. The term "heirloom tomato" refers to a tomato variety that is an open-pollinated (non-hybridized) cultivar of a tomato plant. That means these tomato varieties haven't been scientifically altered to resist diseases, or to grow thicker, stronger skins so they travel better, or been crossed with another variety so they have a longer shelf life. Instead, heirloom tomato varieties have been allowed to continue the way nature planned.

As it turns out, nature is pretty damn smart. Heirloom tomatoes are available in many colours, and each one has its own flavour. The taste differences can be subtle, but they are noticeable if you have perfectly ripe, gently handled tomatoes to taste. That's the main reason I keep the heirloom tomato salad at Pangaea so simple: I want our patrons to really taste the difference in each of these lovely little fruits.

Here are my tips for making a fantastic heirloom tomato salad

---

Choose heirloom tomatoes that have never been refrigerated and store them at room temperature in a shady spot until ready to use.

Slice a variety of different-coloured heirloom tomatoes into disks or wedges just before serving.

Drizzle with a fruity extra virgin olive oil and an excellent quality balsamic vinegar, preferably one that is thick enough to coat the back of a spoon.

Serve with whole, fresh basil leaves or slice basil into a chiffonade and sprinkle over the sliced tomatoes. If serving with buffalo mozzarella, choose one that is young and at or only slightly below room temperature.

Sprinkle salad with sea salt and freshly ground black pepper immediately before eating.

Octopus Salad

Vancouver

Vancouver-based fisherman Steve Johansen supplies us with spot prawns. Steve and I speak often on our cellphones. One day while he was out at sea and I was in my kitchen at Pangaea, I called him to check in on my latest order. He interrupted his answer to curse the "$%*& octopus" that was cluttering up his spot prawn trap.

"What are you going to do with it?" I asked. "Throw the pesky thing back," he replied. I offered to save him the trouble and asked him to send it to me with the rest of my order.

While finding an octopus swimming in his trap is troublesome to Steve, it's great for chefs like me who want to enjoy seafood but don't want to harm the ocean. Octopus hang out on the sea floor, so they're hard to catch without using dredging machinery that harms the plants, coral, and animals that live there. So when one just swims into a trap, it's a lucky occurence.

For this recipe, you can use frozen octopus with no problem. In fact, since freezing weakens the cell walls in the octopus, freezing and thawing it can actually help to tenderize this tough-skinned food.

For 6 servings

Octopus

1.5 lbs (750 g) octopus
8 cups (2 L) cold water
1 cup (250 mL) red wine
1/2 cup (125 mL) red wine vinegar
1/2 cup (125 mL) diced carrot
1/2 cup (125 mL) diced celery
1/2 cup (125 mL) diced onion
1/2 cup (125 mL) diced fennel bulb
6 cloves garlic, crushed
2 tbsp (30 mL) whole black peppercorns
2 tbsp (30 mL) salt

Dressing

1/4 cup (60 mL) Shinmirin (sweet Japanese rice wine, less than 4% alcohol)
1 tbsp (15 mL) rice wine vinegar
1/4 cup (60 mL) red wine vinegar
1 1/2 tsp (7 mL) freshly squeezed lemon juice
Pinch saffron
1 1/2 cups (375 mL) extra virgin olive oil
1/2 cup (125 mL) chopped fresh oregano
3/4 tsp (4 mL) salt
1/2 tsp (2 mL) freshly ground white pepper

Salad

1 red pepper, roasted and peeled (see page 96)
1 yellow pepper, roasted and peeled (see page 96)
1/4 cup (60 mL) julienne strips red onion
1/4 cup (60 mL) halved pitted black Gaeta olives (about 10)
1/4 cup (60 mL) small capers (about half a 4 oz/125 mL jar)
1/4 cup (60 mL) roasted garlic (see page 212)
6 cooked marinated artichokes (see page 211), quartered
1/2 tsp (2 mL) salt or to taste
2 cups (500 mL) mâché or spring mix
Vincotta or balsamic glaze

Octopus

Cut head off of octopus. Fan out octopus legs and cut, like a pie, into eight pieces. Place the octopus in a large saucepan or pasta pot. Fill with the water; add the red wine, red wine vinegar, carrot, celery, onion, fennel, garlic, pepper, and salt. Bring to a boil; reduce the temperature and simmer for 30 to 40 minutes or until octopus is tender enough to puncture with a fork.

Remove pot from the heat and allow the octopus to cool in liquid for at least an hour. Use a clean, damp towel to rub the purple skin from the legs of the octopus but leave suction cups attached and intact. Slice the octopus legs crosswise thinly to make disks. Cover tightly and refrigerate.

Dressing

In a mixing bowl, combine the mirin, rice wine vinegar, red wine vinegar, lemon juice, and saffron. Whisk in the oil. Stir in the oregano, salt, and pepper. Blend thoroughly. Cover tightly and refrigerate for up to 1 week.

Salad

Julienne the roasted peppers. In a bowl, combine the peppers, onion, olives, capers, roasted garlic, and artichokes.

To Assemble

Combine the octopus, salad, and dressing. Toss to combine well. (Mixture can be made to this point and served or covered and marinated in the refrigerator for 2 days.)

To Serve

On six large, round, chilled plates, arrange an equal amount of mâché leaves: Gather all the stems together and fan four bouquets of leaves on the plate so the stem ends meet in the middle and the leaves create a circular bed. Mound 2/3 cup (150 mL) of the octopus mixture inside the lettuce ring. Sprinkle a few drops of the collected juices from the salad around the outside of the mâché, drizzle with a few drops of balsamic glaze, and serve.

Mackerel

is a fish I didn't often choose when Pangaea opened in 1996. But as my understanding of the problems facing the ocean evolved, I realized that quickly maturing fish like mackerel and octopus that produce high numbers of offspring are a good choice for restaurant menus — especially when they taste this good!

For 6 servings

Mackerel
2 whole dressed mackerels, each about 1 lb (500 g)

Braising Liquid
1/2 tsp (2 mL) salt
1 cup (250 mL) white wine vinegar
1 cup (250 mL) dry white wine
1/4 cup (60 mL) diced onion
1/4 cup (60 mL) diced carrot
1/4 cup (60 mL) diced celery
1 bay leaf
1/4 tsp (1 mL) cracked black peppercorns

Barigoule of Vegetables
1 tbsp (15 mL) freshly squeezed lemon juice
9 small whole artichokes
1/4 cup (60 mL) olive oil
1 cup (250 mL) thinly sliced onion
1 cup (250 mL) peeled, thinly sliced carrot
1 bay leaf
2 sprigs fresh thyme
2 tbsp (30 mL) minced garlic, divided
1/2 tsp (2 mL) salt
1/4 tsp (1 mL) freshly ground black pepper or to taste
3/4 cup (175 mL) dry white wine
4 cups (1 L) fish fumet (see page 209)
1/4 tsp (1 mL) saffron
1/2 cup (125 mL) lightly packed fresh basil leaves
12 pieces tomato confit (see page 211)
1/2 cup (125 mL) Gaeta, Niçoise, or other black olives, pitted
1/2 cup (125 mL) coarsely chopped fresh parsley
1 tbsp (30 mL) balsamic vinegar (approx.)
6 sprigs fresh basil

In case you're wondering, barigoule is a traditional Provençal dish that consists of artichokes, onions, garlic, and carrots cooked in a white wine braising liquid. According to my research, the name evolved over time from a dish that featured artichokes stuffed with barigoule mushrooms. Even without the mushrooms, this mixture is still fantastic with mackerel!

Mackerel
Rinse the mackerel inside and out and pat dry. Use a sharp chef's knife to slice just behind the fish's head on an angle. Using smooth, long strokes, run the knife down the body while pressing firmly against the spine. Flip and repeat on the other side. Trim away the rib cage and discard.

Place the boned fish skin-side down. Feeling with your fingertips, remove any pin bones, using tweezers or needle-nose pliers. Slice each fillet on an angle into long pieces each 2 inches (5 cm) wide. Rinse under cold water and pat dry with a paper towel. Reserve in the refrigerator.

Braising Liquid
Combine the salt, vinegar, wine, onion, carrot, and celery in a saucepan. Wrap the bay leaf and peppercorns in cheesecloth and tie closed; add to the saucepan and bring to a boil. Reduce heat and simmer for 10 minutes. Strain and set aside.

Barigoule of Vegetables
Fill a large bowl with about 8 cups (2 L) of cold water and add the lemon juice. Taste

and add more lemon juice if necessary to make the water taste mildly lemony.

To prepare the artichokes, peel away the tough outer leaves until you reach the tender, pale green leaves and the artichoke is bullet-shaped. Cut off the tops and trim the perimeter of the artichoke where the leaves were. Peel and trim the stem of the artichoke, keeping the shape intact. Cut the artichoke in half and submerge in the lemon water.

Heat the olive oil in a deep skillet set over medium-high heat. Add the onion and carrot and sauté, stirring constantly, for 3 to 5 minutes or until lightly browned. Add the bay leaf, thyme, and half the garlic and continue to sauté. When the onions are tender, from 2 to 3 minutes, add the artichokes in a single layer and season with salt and pepper.

Add enough wine and fish fumet to cover the artichokes. Add the saffron and bring to a boil. Reduce to a simmer; cover pan and cook for about 15 minutes. Remove artichokes, set aside, and keep warm. Continue simmering the liquid until reduced by half, about 30 to 40 minutes.

Just prior to serving, remove thyme sprigs and bay leaf from the barigoule mixture and add the halved artichokes, basil leaves, the remaining garlic, the tomato confit, black olives, chopped parsley, and the balsamic vinegar. Taste and add up to 1 tsp (5 mL) more balsamic vinegar if necessary to strike a nice balance. Keep warm.

To Assemble
Preheat the oven to 350°F (180°C). Bring the braising liquid to a boil in a deep skillet or wide saucepan; add the mackerel, skin-side up and overlapping slightly. Transfer to the oven and cook for 4 minutes or until fish flakes easily when tested with a fork. Let stand in the liquid for 3 to 5 minutes.

Place a mound of the vegetables in the centre of a bowl. Sprinkle with salt and pepper. Transfer fish to bowls and discard cooking liquid. Garnish with basil. Serve hot.

Mackerel
Braised in White Wine
on Stewed Barigoule Vegetables

Five Steps to a Perfectly Filleted Fish

At Pangaea we always buy whole fish and clean them ourselves. Follow these steps for cleaning any round fish — Chinook salmon pictured on this page, ocean trout, or lake fish you catch yourself, such as bass.

1. Using a knife with a very sharp, long, thin flexible blade, cut into the fish behind the gills as deeply as the rib cage. Slip the tip of the knife blade under the flesh of the fish just behind the gills. Slide the knife up to the top of the rib cage using clean strokes.

2. Separate the cut fillet from the skeleton of the fish using your free hand. Meanwhile, continue to slide the knife along the side of the fish to slice it from the ribs all the way down to the tail of the fish.

3. After you slice the loosened fillet along the dorsal fin to remove it from the fish, place it flesh-side down on the counter. Use the very tip of the knife to loosen the bottom left corner where the skin attaches to the flesh. Pull up on

this loosened flap with your free hand and hold the skin taut. Smoothly slide the knife between the skin and the flesh using a very small amount of upward pressure to completely and cleanly remove the skin. Discard skin.

4. Turn the fish over and cut away any white or translucent-coloured meat. (Reserve for another use such as making salmon cakes, chowder, or salmon salad.) Using heavy-duty tweezers, remove any visible bones. Run your palm lightly over the fish from the tail end toward the front to find any hidden bones. Remove and discard.

5. Slice fish crosswise into equal-sized portions. If not using immediately, cover tightly and refrigerate for up to 12 hours.

Mahogany

Mahogany-glazed salmon has been on the Pangaea menu since day one. Patrons love it because it's light but still complex and satisfying. When you decide to make it yourself, either buy a side of wild Pacific salmon from your fishmonger or ask them to sell you six skin-on scaled fillets with the pin bones removed. If wild salmon isn't in season, choose a sustainable fish that is.

At Pangaea, we rotate salmon with ocean trout and arctic char, depending on the time of year. You can check to see what fish are recommended as best choices on any given day at seafoodwatch.com. They even have an iPhone application that I have on my phone so I can check availability anytime, anywhere!

Note

You'll find water chestnuts and pickled ginger in most grocery stores and at every Asian market; however, if you have a little extra time, try making your own pickled ginger the way we do at Pangaea. Our recipe is on page 212.

For 6 servings

Salmon
3 lbs (1.5 kg) wild Pacific salmon
1 cup (250 mL) soy sauce
2 tbsp (30 mL) canola oil

Vegetables
6 heads baby bok choy, halved
1 cup (250 mL) peeled, fresh, or canned
    water chestnuts
2 cups (500 mL) shiitake mushroom caps
1 tbsp (15 mL) butter
1 tbsp (15 mL) canola oil
1/2 cup (125 mL) diced red onion
1 tsp (5 mL) minced garlic
1/4 cup (60 mL) sliced pickled ginger,
    drained, divided
Salt and freshly ground black pepper

Caramel Lime Butter
1/4 cup (60 mL) granulated sugar
1/4 cup (60 mL) water
3 tbsp (45 mL) freshly squeezed lime juice
1 cup (250 mL) chilled cubed butter
1/2 tsp (2 mL) salt
1/4 tsp (1 mL) freshly ground white pepper

Salmon

If using a side of salmon, scale and then fillet the salmon (see page 105). Remove any stray pin bones. Cut the salmon into 6 portions and arrange in a single layer in a casserole or non-reactive roasting pan. Pour soy sauce over salmon fillets and turn to coat. Place in the refrigerator for at least 1 hour or for up to 4 hours.

Vegetables

Wash the bok choy under cold running water until completely grit free. Plunge into boiling salted water and cook for 2 minutes. Drain and transfer the bok choy to an ice bath. Chill completely; drain well. Place on a tray and reserve in refrigerator.

Slice the water chestnuts into thin rounds and place in cold water. Wipe the mushroom caps clean with a slightly damp cloth; slice each mushroom into thin strips.

Caramel Lime Butter

In a small saucepan set over medium-high heat, combine the sugar and water; bring to a boil. Reduce the liquid for 5 minutes or until it forms a topaz-coloured caramel.

Standing so that your face and body are out of splatter range, add the lime juice (the caramel will harden and look split for a few moments and then liquefy as it cooks) and continue to cook for an additional minute. Remove the lime-caramel mixture from the heat and cool slightly.

Reduce the heat to low and return the mixture to the stovetop (this is to temper the caramel mixture slightly so that the butter doesn't split when you begin adding it). Using a whisk with fine, flexible tines, slowly whisk in the cold butter, one piece at a time; whisk until almost completely incorporated. Season with salt and pepper and keep warm.

To Assemble

Preheat the oven to 350°F (180°C). Heat the oil in a large skillet set over medium heat. Remove the salmon from the marinade and pat dry on paper towel. Place fish in the pan skin-side down; cook for 3 to 4 minutes or until browned; turn and repeat. Transfer the salmon to the oven and cook for 5 minutes or until salmon is firm but still slightly translucent in the centre.

While the salmon cooks, prepare the vegetables: Melt the butter with the oil in a skillet set over medium-high heat. When the butter begins to foam, add the onions and sauté until soft. Next add the mushrooms and sauté until soft and slightly caramelized. Add the water chestnuts, garlic, reserved bok choy, and half the pickled ginger. Cook, stirring, until bok choy is heated through. Season with salt and pepper.

Divide the vegetable mixture evenly and use a portion to make a nest in the centre of each of six serving plates. Top each nest with a piece of salmon, skin side up. Using about 1 tsp (5 mL) of pickled ginger for each plate, form rosettes and place next to vegetables. Drizzle sauce around salmon and serve.

Mahogany-Glazed Wild Salmon, Wilted Bok Choy, Water Chestnuts, Shiitake Mushrooms, and Lime Caramel Sauce

Tips

Remove the stems from shiitake mushrooms by using either a small knife or by pinching the stem under the cap and twisting. You can reserve the stems for soup or stocks.

You can also grill the salmon. Use a wire brush to scrape the grill clean. Preheat to medium-high. When the grill is hot, wipe the grate with a cloth soaked in vegetable oil. (Be careful of any flare-ups from the oil!) Coat the salmon with a little vegetable oil and grill, skin-side down, for 4 minutes. Rotate the salmon 90 degrees and cook for 3 more minutes. Turn the salmon and repeat.

It's **mind-boggling** to imagine that bison (buffalo) herds used to roam the plains south of the Great Lakes and greatly outnumbered the people. While herds of wood bison still live in the northwestern part of Canada, the bison we cook at Pangaea is raised on a farm specifically to be consumed as a food product.

For 6 servings

Bison

½ cup (125 mL) fresh or thawed frozen
   wild blueberries
1 tsp (5 mL) red wine vinegar
1 whole star anise
½ tsp (2 mL) ground cinnamon
1 tbsp (15 mL) buckwheat or organic
   liquid honey
¼ tsp (1 mL) salt
6 California-cut (see note, page 109) bison
   strip loin steaks, 6 oz (175 g) each
1 tbsp (15 mL) canola oil
¾ cup (175 mL) veal reduction (see page 210)

Celeriac Purée

4 cups (1 L) peeled, diced celeriac, about 1 lb
   (500 g)
1½ cups (375 mL) peeled, cored, diced
   Granny Smith apples
4 cups (1 L) whole (homogenized) milk
1 tbsp (15 mL) butter
¾ tsp (4 mL) salt
Pinch freshly ground white pepper

Kale

2 bunches curly kale, about 1½ lbs
   (750 g) in total
1 tbsp (15 mL) unsalted butter
⅓ cup (75 mL) diced white onion
1 tsp (5 mL) minced garlic
1 tsp (5 mL) minced jalapeño pepper
1 tsp (5 mL) chopped fresh thyme leaves
2 tsp (1 mL) cider vinegar
½ tsp (2 mL) salt or to taste
½ tsp (2 mL) freshly ground white pepper
   or to taste

Bison has dark-coloured flesh and a moist, rich texture even when cooked beyond medium doneness. As a result, cooks first experimenting with bison often overcook it and then find it tough. Like many of the other meat recipes in this book, my bison cooking method creates cooked meat with an even, perfect colour that other people use sous-vide thermal circulators to achieve. My method is a bit unusual but worth using when you're cooking a premium cut of meat.

Bison has many culinary advantages and some strong nutritional benefits over other red meats. Compared with beef, for instance, it's much leaner and considerably lower in calories.

Bison

Combine the blueberries, red wine vinegar, star anise, cinnamon, honey, and salt in a small stainless-steel saucepan. Place over high heat and bring to a boil. Reduce heat to a simmer and reduce the liquid by one-quarter. Remove the star anise and place blueberry mixture into a blender or food processor; purée until smooth. Strain cooked blueberry mixture through a fine-mesh sieve and cool to room temperature. Chill completely.

Pat the bison between paper towels. Coat each piece of bison with 1 tbsp (15 mL) of the chilled blueberry mixture; place on a ceramic plate, cover with plastic wrap, and refrigerate for at least 2 hours or for up to 24 hours.

Preheat oven to 350°F (180°C). Remove the bison from the plate and pat dry. In a skillet set over medium heat, heat the oil and wait for it to begin smoking. Place the bison in the pan and brown on all four sides until golden brown, about 5 minutes. Rest the meat on a cutting board for 10 minutes. Transfer the bison back to the pan and roast in the preheated oven for 10 minutes, turning once, for rare (which is what I recommend for this ultra-lean meat) or for 15 minutes for medium-rare. Remove the bison and brush with remaining blueberry glaze; rest for an additional 10 minutes before slicing thinly across the grain.

Celeriac Purée

In a saucepan, combine the celeriac, apples, and milk. Bring to a boil; reduce the heat to a simmer and cook until the celeriac is fork tender, from 10 to 12 minutes. Remove from the heat; drain, reserving the cooking liquid. Transfer the celeriac mixture to a food processor and blend until smooth, adding as much of the reserved cooking liquid as needed to create a smooth texture, about 1 cup (250 mL). Stir in the butter and season with salt and white pepper. (Can be made up to 1 day ahead and reheated just before serving.)

Kale

Remove the stems and centre ribs from each kale leaf and tear the leaves into strips. Cook the kale in a large pot of boiling salted water, using a wooden spoon to ensure the kale remains submerged, for 3 to 5 minutes or until tender. Drain and transfer the kale to an ice bath, chill, then drain well. Gently squeeze the excess moisture from the kale and pat dry.

In a large skillet set over medium heat, melt the butter. Once the butter foams, add the onions and sauté for 1 minute. Add the garlic and jalapeño and sauté for an additional minute or until the garlic begins to brown slightly. Add the kale and toss well, using a spoon to mix the onions in well. When the kale is hot, add the thyme and vinegar. Taste and season the kale with salt and white pepper.

Bison with Wild Blueberry Sauce,
Celeriac, and Wilted Curly Kale

To Assemble
Heat the veal reduction thoroughly. Place ¹/₂ cup (125 mL) of celeriac purée in the centre of six warmed plates. With the back of a spoon, form a well in the centre or the purée and divide the kale evenly into each. Top with a portion of bison, drizzle a little veal reduction around the celeriac, and serve at once.

Note
California-cut strip loin steaks are becoming more popular but are still unusual even in restaurants. Basically, instead of cutting a whole strip loin crosswise into diamond-shaped steaks, butchers and chefs cut the whole strip loin lengthwise first, to make two halves, and then cut thicker steaks from each of these long pieces. This cut is perfect for bison because they have a different body shape than beef cattle and as a result smaller loins.

Fresh corn

is highlighted in this summer dish. Corn is one of our most anticipated local harvests. It's not uncommon to hear people talking about their weekend pilgrimages to farmers' markets to get the first sweet, sunshiny yellow cobs. Invariably, debates over what variety of corn is sweetest, juiciest, and most delicious pop up. And these chats can become time-consuming, since there are literally dozens of varieties of sweet corn grown near here, including Miracle, Kandy Korn, Earlyvee, Flavorvee, Escalade, Silver Queen, Phenomenal, Seneca, Champ, Horizon, and Extra Early Supersweet. For me, while the variety is not unimportant, freshness is the essential factor in choosing corn. Ideally, I like to cook corn the same day it's been picked so the natural sugars haven't turned to starch.

Also used in this recipe are Cornish hens, a hybrid of Cornish and White Rock chickens that are much smaller than a normal broiler or fryer. I'm well practised and don't mind deboning these birds; however, feel free to substitute boneless, skin-on chicken breasts, instead. Just be sure to cook them until the juices run clear.

For 6 servings

Cornish Hens
3 Cornish hens, each 1½ lbs (750 g)
Salt and freshly ground black pepper
2 tbsp (30 mL) canola oil

Corn Fritters
Oil for deep-fryer
1 cup (250 mL) fresh corn kernels, 2 small cobs
1 tsp (5 mL) minced garlic
½ cup (125 mL) fresh coriander, chopped
½ tsp (2 mL) chopped fresh red Thai chile pepper, about 1 to 2 peppers (depending on size)
½ cup (125 mL) green onion, sliced
1 tbsp (15 mL) soy sauce
½ cup (125 mL) all-purpose flour (approx.)
¼ cup (60 mL) rice flour or additional all-purpose flour
2 eggs, lightly beaten
¼ cup (60 mL) water
½ tsp (2 mL) salt
½ tsp (2 mL) freshly ground black pepper

Maple-Chile Sauce
1 cup (250 mL) pure maple syrup
1 tbsp (15 mL) cider vinegar
1 tbsp (15 mL) dry sherry
1 tbsp (15 mL) soy sauce
1 tbsp (15 mL) minced fresh ginger
1 tbsp (15 mL) minced garlic
1 fresh red Thai chile pepper, split lengthwise
Pinch freshly ground white pepper
Pinch hot or mild smoked paprika

Garnish (optional)
Fresh coriander sprigs

Cornish Hens
Wash hens and pat dry. Fully debone each hen: Position the hen breast-side up, legs pointing toward you. Using a sharp knife with a flexible tip, make a long incision on either side of the breastbone. With smooth, even strokes, slide the tip of the knife under the breast to separate the meat from the rib cage and wishbone. Use your thumb to pull the meat away from the bones as you move the knife down the rib cage.

Slice down along the backbone to separate one half of the flesh from the carcass. Twist the wing and leg joints to dislocate. Cut off the wing tip. Locate the drumette and cut around the base that is closest to the breast. Pull the meat away toward the tip to remove the cartilage and expose the clean drumette bone. Repeat on the opposite side.

Run a knife along either side of the leg bone to separate from meat. Pinch and lift the lower section of the drumstick and slide the knife between the meat and bone to separate; repeat with thigh section of bone.

Slide the knife between the meat and remaining connected joint to release the bone completely. Remove bone. Repeat on the opposite side.

Trim and discard any loose, long skin attached to the fully boned hen. Check for any remaining bones or cartilage and remove carefully. Reserve bones for stock.

Repeat with each game hen. When finished, you will have 6 flat, boned pieces of meat. Spread meat on a paper towel–lined platter and pat dry. Reserve in the refrigerator.

Corn Fritters
Preheat a deep-fryer filled with oil per manufacturer's instructions to 350°F (180°C). Mix the corn with the garlic, coriander, chile peppers, green onion, soy sauce, all-purpose flour, rice flour (if using), eggs, and water. Season with salt and pepper and mix thoroughly. The mixture should be firm enough to hold its shape loosely; if required, add a little more flour.

Divide the mixture into 18 equal portions, each about 1 mounded tablespoon (15 mL). Use two spoons to shape each portion into an oval.

Working in batches, gently lower each portion to the oil in a spoon and slide it into the hot oil. Cook for 3 to 5 minutes or until golden; drain on paper towels and keep warm, uncovered, until needed. Bring the oil back to 350°F (180°C) before adding another batch of fritters. Fritters can be made ahead and reheated in the oil just before serving.

Maple-Chili Sauce
In a saucepan, combine the maple syrup, vinegar, sherry, soy sauce, ginger, garlic, chile pepper, pepper, and paprika. Bring to a boil; reduce the heat and simmer for 20 to 25 minutes or until reduced by half. Remove chile and discard. Serve sauce warm.

Cornish Hens with Corn Fritters and Maple-Chile Sauce

To Assemble

Preheat oven to 350°F (180°C). Season the Cornish hens on both sides with salt and pepper.

In a skillet set over medium heat, heat the oil for 1 to 2 minutes or until very hot. Add the Cornish game hens, skin-side down, and sear for 4 minutes; turn once and sear for 2 more minutes. Transfer to a metal baking sheet and bake in the preheated oven for 9 minutes. Remove and let rest for 8 minutes before serving.

When done, cut the skin separating the leg from the breast and stack, skin-side up, with the breast on top of the leg. Place one stack on the bottom half of a heated plate (you'll need six). Place a folded cocktail napkin on the plate and place 3 corn fritters on top of it. Fill six small ramekins with the Maple-Chile Sauce and serve beside the fritters. Garnish the plate with a sprig of coriander if desired.

Tip

An average cob of corn should yield about ³/₄ cup (175 mL) of kernels. To remove kernels from cob, cut the stalk end of the cob flat. Stand cob on this end and hold cob with one hand. Use a sharp, heavy knife to slice down the sides of the cob to remove the kernels.

Wild blueberries,

hand-picked amid the exposed granite contours of the Canadian Shield, and fresh, sunshine-kissed Niagara peaches are featured in this dessert, epitomizing the best an Ontario summer has to offer. And that's not just my opinion. *Toronto Life* magazine highlighted this dessert as one of the top 100 things everyone should try during their lifetime!

Most years, the peaches and blueberries aren't simultaneously perfect until early August; however, as early as mid-July we start getting calls from patrons asking, "Is it time yet?" Hold on to this recipe until both are in season in your area!

For 8 servings

Peach-Ginger Sorbet
1-inch (2.5 cm) piece fresh ginger
1 cup (250 mL) water
²/₃ cup (150 mL) granulated sugar
1 tbsp (15 mL) freshly squeezed lime juice
¼ cup (60 mL) white corn syrup
4 cups (1 L) sliced, pitted, peeled peaches, about 1¼ lbs (600 g)
2 tbsp (30 mL) vitamin C powder (ascorbic acid powder) or Fruit-Fresh

Tart Pastry
½ cup (125 mL) cold butter, cubed
¼ cup (60 mL) granulated sugar
1 egg yolk
2 tbsp (30 mL) whipping (35%) cream
1½ cups (375 mL) all-purpose flour (approx.)
Pinch salt

Vanilla Pastry Cream
1 cup (250 mL) whole (homogenized) milk
½ vanilla bean, scraped
⅓ cup (75 mL) granulated sugar, divided
3 egg yolks
2 tbsp (30 mL) cornstarch, sifted

Topping
4½ cups (1.25 L) fresh wild blueberries, divided
¾ cup (175 mL) granulated sugar
2 tbsp (30 mL) cornstarch, sifted
½ cup (125 mL) water (approx.)
2 tsp (10 mL) freshly squeezed lemon juice

Garnish (optional)
Fresh mint leaves

Peach-Ginger Sorbet
Peel the ginger and slice very thinly. Place in a saucepan with the water, sugar, lime juice, and corn syrup. Set over high heat and bring to a boil. Remove from heat and cool to room temperature. Strain the liquid into a high-speed blender and discard the ginger.

Add the peaches and vitamin C powder (ascorbic acid powder) to the blender and purée until very smooth. Chill completely. Transfer to an ice cream machine and freeze according to manufacturer's instructions.

Tart Pastry
Combine the butter and sugar in the bowl of an electric stand mixer fitted with a paddle attachment. Blend on medium speed for 1 minute or until the ingredients are well combined. In a small bowl, whisk together the egg yolk and cream; add to the butter mixture and mix until incorporated.

Scrape down the sides of the bowl with a rubber spatula. Add the flour and salt and mix on low speed for 1 minute or until a dough forms. Transfer to a clean work surface lightly dusted with flour and knead gently into a smooth ball. Flatten into a disk and wrap tightly in plastic wrap. Chill for 2 hours or until firm.

Roll out dough on a clean work surface lightly dusted with flour. Use a 4-inch (10 cm) round cutter to cut. Press into and halfway up the sides of eight individual tart or pie rings. Line each tart with parchment paper and pie weights. Refrigerate for at least 30 minutes.

Preheat the oven to 350°F (180°C). Bake tart shells for 20 minutes. Cool slightly. Remove the weights, paper, and tart ring. Return to oven and bake for 15 to 20 minutes or until pale gold. Cool completely.

Vanilla Pastry Cream
Place the milk in a saucepan. Add the vanilla bean and the scraped seeds; whisk in half of the sugar. Set over medium-high heat. Heat until bubbles begin to form around the edge of the pan and the milk just begins to bubble. Remove pan from heat.

Quickly, beat the eggs with the remaining sugar and the sifted cornstarch until very smooth. Whisk a little of the hot milk into the mixture until smooth. Scrape the egg mixture into the saucepan using a rubber spatula.

Cook, whisking constantly, for 2 minutes or until the custard is smooth and very thick. Remove and discard vanilla bean pod. Transfer to mixing bowl and cover with plastic wrap touching the surface of the custard. Cool to room temperature. Transfer to an airtight container and refrigerate. Just before serving, beat using an electric mixer fitted with a whisk attachment, until very smooth.

Topping
Pick over the berries, removing any stems or withered fruit. Place ½ cup (125 mL) of the berries in a small skillet. Toss to combine with the sugar and cornstarch. Mash the berries with the back of a wooden spoon. Stir in the water and set over medium heat. Cook, stirring constantly, for 5 minutes or until the mixture thickens and becomes glossy and dark. Stir in the lemon juice.

To Assemble
Fill each baked tart shell with an equal amount of the vanilla pastry cream. Scrape

the hot blueberry mixture over the remaining berries. Gently fold the berries together until they are all evenly coated but some of the bloom is still visible on the raw berries. Spoon equal amounts of the blueberry mixture over the pastry cream in each tart, mounding the berries in the centre. Cool until set.

To serve, place a tart and a scoop of Peach-Ginger Sorbet on each serving plate. Garnish with mint, if using.

Tip
To prepare peaches, score an X in the bottom of each piece of fruit using a sharp paring knife. Blanch peaches in boiling water for 15 seconds. Drain well and plunge into ice water. Slip skins off using your fingers; halve peaches and remove and discard pit.

Wild Blueberry Tart with Peach-Ginger Sorbet and Mint

This dessert

is a tribute to the Niagara Peninsula, which is internationally renowned not only for its award-winning wine production but also for producing fantastic tree fruit, including 90% of the apricots, nectarines, and peaches grown in Ontario. Since we're only a 90-minute drive from these orchards, apricots from that region can be picked at full ripeness and arrive in our kitchen in perfect condition.

The most famous Niagara product is ice wine and in this dessert, it's turned into a boozy ice cream that complements in-season apricots perfectly!

For 6 servings

Ice Wine Ice Cream
1 cup (250 mL) whipping (35%) cream
1 cup (250 mL) whole (homogenized) milk
1/3 cup (75 mL) granulated sugar, divided
5 egg yolks
1 cup (250 mL) ice wine or late harvest Vidal

Poached Apricots
3 cups (750 mL) water
1 cup (250 mL) granulated sugar
1/2 cup (125 mL) liquid honey
1/2 vanilla bean, scraped
1 tbsp (15 mL) vitamin C powder (ascorbic acid powder) or Fruit-Fresh
9 ripe apricots, halved and pitted

Cornmeal Upside-Down Cakes
18 poached apricot halves (see above)
9 large blackberries, halved lengthwise
1/2 vanilla bean, halved lengthwise
1/4 cup (60 mL) butter, softened
9 tbsp (135 mL) granulated sugar, divided
2 eggs, separated
3/4 cup (175 mL) all-purpose flour
4 tsp (20 mL) fine cornmeal
3/4 tsp (4 mL) baking powder
1/4 tsp (1 mL) salt
1/3 cup (75 mL) whole (homogenized) milk
2 tbsp (30 mL) apple jelly
Mint (optional)
Confectioners' (icing) sugar

Garnish (optional)
Fresh mint sprigs
Blackberry Compote (see page 158)

Ice Wine Ice Cream
Combine the cream, milk, and half the sugar in a saucepan. Place over medium-high heat and heat until mixture just comes to a boil.

Meanwhile, combine the remaining sugar and eggs, whisking until smooth. Pour a little of the hot milk mixture into the bowl and whisk well. Transfer the egg mixture to the saucepan, scraping every bit into the pan with a rubber spatula. Cook, stirring constantly, over medium-high heat for 1 minute or until the mixture coats the back of a spoon well. Strain mixture into a clean container and whisk in ice wine. Chill completely.

Transfer the chilled mixture to an ice cream machine and churn according to manufacturer's instructions. Transfer to a tub that seals tightly and freeze until set enough to scoop.

Poached Apricots
Combine the water, sugar, honey, vanilla bean and its scraped seeds, and the vitamin C powder in a large saucepan. Place over high heat and bring to a boil. Add the apricots and cover the surface of the pan with a parchment paper cartouche (see note, page 189).

Remove from the heat and let apricots cool, submerged in the syrup, to room temperature.

Cornmeal Upside-Down Cakes
Preheat the oven to 350°F (180°C). Arrange 3 apricot halves, skin-side down, in one of six 4-oz (125 mL) dome-shaped silicone baking cups or jumbo muffin tins. Nestle 3 of blackberry halves between the apricots in each dome, making sure the cut side faces the inside of the pan.

Scrape the seeds from the vanilla bean; transfer the seeds to the bowl of a stand mixer fitted with the paddle attachment. Add the butter and all but 1 tbsp (15 mL) of the sugar; beat until light and fluffy. Add the egg yolks one at a time and beat well. Scrape down the bowl.

Sift the flour with the cornmeal, baking powder, and salt. Mixing on low speed, add the dry ingredients alternating with the milk, scraping down the bowl as needed.

In a clean mixing bowl, using a clean whisk attachment, beat the egg whites with the remaining 1 tbsp (15 mL) sugar on high until soft peaks form. Using a rubber spatula, fold the egg whites into the cake batter. Divide the batter evenly between the prepared baking cups. Smooth the top of each cake.

Bake in the preheated oven for 30 to 35 minutes or until a tester inserted in the centre of one of the cakes comes out clean. Cool on a rack for 5 minutes. Place a sheet of parchment paper over the cakes. Top with a baking sheet and a weight, such as a can of tomatoes; let stand for 20 minutes to ensure that the cakes have flat bottoms. Remove tray and let cakes cool completely before running a knife around the edge of each cake and unmoulding. Heat the apple jelly until melted. Using a pastry brush, lightly brush over the top of each cake.

To Assemble
Dust six plates with confectioners' sugar. Place a cake, fruit-side up, on each plate. Place a scoop of Ice Wine Ice Cream off to one side. Garnish with a sprig of mint if desired. If you like, add another fruity dimension by garnishing this dessert with the Blackberry Compote featured on page 158.

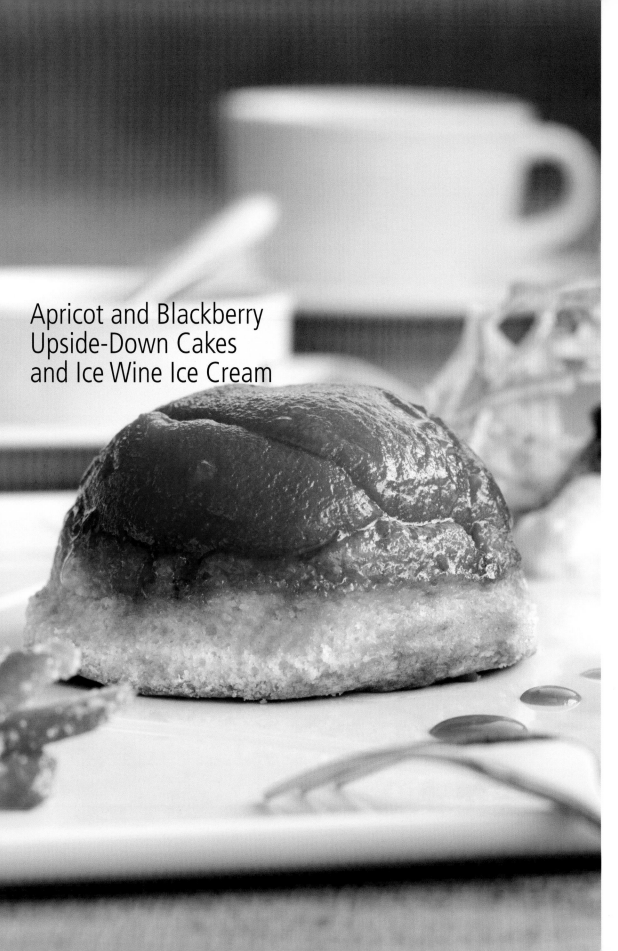

Apricot and Blackberry Upside-Down Cakes and Ice Wine Ice Cream

Note
Colen Quinn, our pastry chef, zips up Bay Street to Markie's Pharmacy to buy pure vitamin C powder to add to the apricot poaching liquid because it is all-natural and prevents the fruit from browning; however, I always suspect she just wants a breath of summer air, since we could easily order Fruit-Fresh crystals from our dry goods supplier and they'd do the same job. Feel free to use whichever product is easiest for you to find, but please don't add lemon juice to prevent browning — in this dessert, the pure apricot flavour is just too good to alter.

*Cake in picture to left made with Fuji apples. Simply substitute the apricots with 8 apples if apricots are out of season.

Autumn

Bringing Back Local Chestnuts

I first encountered chestnuts and learned to appreciate them as an ingredient when I was immersed in classical French cuisine as a young chef in Quebec. I spent hours peeling cases of fresh chestnuts under the scrutinizing eye of my chef, Robert Bourassa, who was an excellent teacher with a perfectionist's standards. He expected every bit of bitter skin to be removed before one of us poached the peeled nutmeats in game broth, to be used as a garnish for venison and duck dishes.

Although my fingertips were raw by the time the job was complete, I was smitten. There was just no way to resist the allure of chestnuts; their vaguely sweet, starchy flavour was worth every effort. In fact, tasting a fresh, properly prepared chestnut spoiled my palate so that I could no longer face canned chestnut purées that taste more like tin-flavoured mush than food.

As I rose through the ranks to hold more responsible kitchen positions where I was expected to plan menus and order ingredients, I learned that we're lucky to have access to Canadian chestnuts at all.

Although the American chestnut tree was common in Canadian woodlands a century ago, sadly, in 1904 a pernicious fungal blight decimated our native chestnut forests.

This blight attacked the bark and cambium of the twigs, branches, and main trunk of chestnut trees and continues to prevent these stately hardwoods from flourishing.

Fortunately, there are people working to eradicate this problem and nurture our native chestnut trees back to health any way they can. Grove keepers like Niagara-on-the-Lake's Ernie Grimo (left) are developing solutions for controlling blight and are producing Canadian-grown chestnuts in limited amounts. Until the blight is eradicated, however, we'll never have a plentiful supply. That's why Ernie has developed not only unique growing techniques but also an excellent dehydrating method that preserves the harvest in a way that ensures chefs can count on good culinary results for many months after the fresh chestnuts are gone.

At Pangaea, I use Ernie's fresh and dehydrated chestnuts in dishes such as the caribou dish on page 150. It's being able to create these wonderful flavour combinations that continues to inspire me to work harder as a chef.

Cheval

Depending on how well you paid attention in your high school French class, you may have already guessed that this section is about horsemeat (called *cheval, en français*). In 2008 I was courting controversy when I served glistening mounds of horsemeat tartar on succulent Cookstown Greens dahlia root at the second annual Picnic at the Brick Works, an event hosted by the Evergreen Foundation and Slow Food Toronto. I was very surprised by the reaction to my offering. While a few people demurred, most of the guests were inquisitive enough to try my recipe, and almost everyone who sampled the cheval tartar proclaimed it delicious.

During my apprenticeship as a cook at Café Henry Burger in Hull, Quebec, I learned how to prepare horsemeat in many ways. Its lean, close, compact texture and underlying sweet flavour are very satisfying and make a terrific tartar.

Unfortunately, what I didn't know when I put horsemeat on the menu at Pangaea — and then served it at the Brick Works picnic — is that most of the product currently for sale in Canada isn't raised as food. That means that the quality varies widely and there's no assurance that the meat being

served was raised without exposure to drugs or hormones. I'm very cautious when I purchase meat, so when there is a chance that the meat I purchase could be a 12-year-old ex-racehorse that was pumped full of medications for its whole life, the supply just doesn't meet my quality criteria.

As I write this book, I'm lobbying for a grading system to be established so that poorer-quality horsemeat is streamed out of the food system to become pet food while less tender, medically verified advanced-age horses can be graded as appropriate for making more rustic foods, such as cold cuts like bresaola and salami. It's my hope that creating a grading system will encourage more farmers to raise purpose-bred culinary horsemeat. Ideally, horsemeat farms should operate similarly to the ones from which we now buy our beef, pork, chicken, and game meats, such as venison and duck.

While I'm waiting for the Canadian horsemeat industry to adopt a horsemeat grading system, you and I can make the horsemeat recipe on page 156 using beef. In the meantime, if you find yourself in Japan, where I understand great-quality purpose-bred horsemeat — custom raised in Canada! — is available, you can make my horsemeat tartar recipe as written.

Liv(er)ing
It Up!

Driving up to La Ferme Palmex's brood farm on a sunny summer morning is the kind of experience you want to memorize and pull out to console your winter-weary soul around February when it seems that warm sunshine and green grass will never return. It's just that tranquil.

The farm is run by Margaret, a fresh-faced young woman who gathers the eggs and ensures that the several hundred mother ducks in her care are well fed and content. She and the ducks divide their time between two aluminum-clad barns nestled between the rounded peaks of Mont Saint-Hilaire and Mont Rougemont in Quebec's Montérégie area. It's a lovely setting not only to be a duck but also to be a person.

I made a point of visiting the brood farm and also the finishing barn and processing plant where the foie de canard and Mullard duck breasts and legs we use at Pangaea are butchered and packaged. Foie gras and foie de canard are controversial, so I wanted to be sure that I was getting great-quality products from animals that were raised as humanely as possible.

The process of creating foie gras and foie de canard is often criticized for being cruel; however, it occurs each year in nature when geese and ducks gorge themselves to build the fat reserves in their livers and subcutaneous tissues that will nourish them when they migrate to warmer climates. For culinary use, web-footed birds are fattened using a process called gavage, which changes their eating pattern. Before the gavage process begins, ducks are allowed to eat and drink whenever they like. Two weeks before gavage commences, their caregivers give them just one meal each day in which they receive 8 ounces (250 g) of food. As a result of this feeding regime, the ducks' crops (the expanded, muscular pouches near the bird's gullet, or throat, that is used to store food temporarily) begin to open up so that gavage can be comfortable.

That's when the ducks are transferred to the gavage barn I toured with the president of Palmex, Benoit Couchet, and Pascal Fleury, the consultant in charge of animal welfare. (Pascal started out as a corn farmer in France and learned about duck keeping and foie de

canard production there, as well.) It was a fascinating morning watching Pascal and his two barn hands carefully regulating the temperature and humidity of the barn so the ducks were always comfortable. Then they tested the pH content of the water to make sure it was no more and no less than 7.5 because at this level the water blends well with the ground-corn-based feed the ducks eat and is easily digested. Last, they checked each bird to make sure their crops were open. (If necessary, Pascal's team will modify an individual duck's diet to ensure that, as the liver grows, the duck is comfortable and healthy.)

The biggest surprise I had on my tour was realizing how nonplussed the ducks were to see and be fed with the embuc, or funnel. I'd always worried about that part of the process, yet it was obviously not a problem for the birds! Likewise, the feeding time was incredibly short. It took literally less than 10 seconds for Pascal to feed each bird with the fountain-pen-thick electric embuc.

It required a long drive, but visiting this supplier was particularly gratifying. There are a lot of reasons I feel good about using Benoit and Pascal's foie de canard in my terrine and other recipes. They encourage their customers to learn about the gavage process and to understand how to assess quality. For instance, they encourage chefs to choose the smaller livers, which take less time to produce than the larger livers that some North American companies recommend. That means the ducks spend less time in the gavage barn and the foie de canard is better-quality, rendering less melted fat when it's cooked. That seems like a good thing for the birds and for my bottom line!

My partner, Peter Geary, visited another farm farther north, in Quebec's Charlevoix region, that raises free-range geese that are barn-finished to produce foie gras. Their foie gras was fantastic, but we chose to go with Palmex, not only because they are closer to Toronto (foie gras and foie de canard, like fish, are best when they're fresh) but also because they can supply duck liver to us consistently from a federally inspected plant.

Truffles: Sniffing Out the Best

If you've ever seen a truffle up close, you may wonder what the fuss is all about. At best, truffles resemble little lumps, and at worst — well, that's better left unsaid. However, it's not how truffles look but how they smell and taste that are the true selling points of these curious little tubers.

It's no use to shyly describe their aroma as earthy; the appeal of truffles hinges on their sex appeal. That's right, sex. Truffles prove the point that advertisers have been making for years: Sex sells. Truffles are rich in the natural chemical testosterase, which has a very similar chemical composition to testosterone, the hormone that lends human semen its characteristic smell. This sexy smell drives sows mad and makes them ideal animals for locating truffles — the smell acts as an aphrodisiac, causing the pigs to want to locate truffles with incredible urgency.

The aroma affects humans much more subtly, but it still elicits a voluptuous, sensuous response. Being more than 73% water, truffles have very little nutrient value and are appealing as a food almost solely because of their unique taste and perfume. And unlike many other luxury foods, truffles are low-fat, low-cholesterol, and low-sodium — the perfect gift for anyone you want to keep around for a long time!

Even more mysterious than the subliminal appeal of truffles is the way truffles grow. Truffles live in a symbiotic relationship with a number of hardwood trees, such as hickories and oaks. Trees with truffles growing beneath them often look stunted or have slightly mounded bases pushed up by the truffles and hyphae growing beneath the surface. Hyphae, a non-edible plant, grow in a network of threads that reach many feet (metres) into the ground and interact with the tree roots that provide carbohydrates for this plant and the truffles to grow. Although truffles are the fruit of the hyphae plant, they quite mysteriously seem to have no physical stem, vine, or other attachment to it.

I buy white truffles, which come into season before black truffles, from Wanda Sdroc of whitetruffles.ca, as mentioned on page 23. White truffles mature in autumn and can weigh from 2 ounces (30 g) to 2 pounds (1 kg)! They are very delicate, losing about 5% of their body weight per day due to dehydration. As a result, white truffles must be treated with care and used quickly. Try to slice them and serve them raw, since heating, grating, or compressing white truffles destroys their flavour.

Unlike other distributors, who are often the third or fourth person in the import chain, Wanda's truffles are harvested from the forests that surround her family's land along the Mirna River in northern Croatia — an area many gastronomes are calling "the new Tuscany" because the climate and produce are so similar — and arrive incredibly fresh.

"We use golden retrievers to help us locate first-grade truffles. Although the legal, internationally agreed upon beginning of the truffle trading season is September 15, we begin our harvest a couple of weeks later, when the truffles are more mature and better able to travel without losing their perfume and quality," notes Srdoc.

I don't recommend most of the commercially available truffle oils on the market because they're made with synthetic truffle essence, but I do often buy Wanda's organic truffle oil, made with extra virgin olive oil pressed from the fruit grown in her grandmother's centuries-old olive grove. Wanda's family infuses real white truffles in the oil using a special mixing machine purchased in Italy.

Later in the season, when the white truffles are over, I switch to black (Perigord) truffles. The interior of these "black diamonds" is actually a deep violet or burgundy colour with tiny white veins traversing through the flesh; the exterior is rough and black. Regardless of the colour, store truffles for as short a time as possible. They can be stored at home in several ways: tightly wrapped on a bed of rice to retain moisture or in an airtight container filled with eggs or butter (which will be infused with the flavour of the truffles!), or wrapped in paper towel and then sealed in an airtight container.

Autumn
recipes

Appetizers

Main Courses

Desserts

Triptych of Autumn Soups
    Cauliflower with Saffron and Cinnamon
    Beet and Apple Cider with Curried Walnuts
    Spiced Pumpkin with Pear

Beets, pumpkins, and cauliflower are a congenial trio that complement one another well as flavours and as colours. Pangaea's autumn soup triptychs often showcase these vegetables.

From fruit to sweet spices like cinnamon, these soups all have a soft flavour element that tempers assertive spices such as saffron, curry, or cloves. As a result, they all have a warming note that is perfect for this time of year when the days are cool and crisp. However, these spices can mellow to the point of dullness after a couple of days of being added to a dish. So, I advise that if you make these soups ahead, that you taste each one after reheating and adjust the spices and seasonings before serving.

For 8 servings each of three soups

Cauliflower Soup with Saffron and Cinnamon

1 tbsp (15 mL) butter
¼ cup (60 mL) finely diced white onion
¼ tsp (1 mL) ground cinnamon
¼ cup (60 mL) white wine
3 cups (750 mL) diced cauliflower
Pinch saffron
1 bay leaf
3½ cups (875 mL) chicken stock (see page 208)
¾ tsp (4 mL) salt or to taste
1 tbsp (15 mL) blanched cauliflower florets for garnish

To Serve
Warm three small bowls per person. Spoon out even portions of the three soups and garnish with appropriate toppings.

Tips
If a soup thickens as it sits, adjust the texture by adding a little boiling water.

For vegetarian versions, substitute vegetable broth or water for the chicken stock.

Cauliflower Soup with Saffron and Cinnamon
In a saucepan set over medium heat, melt the butter. Once the butter begins to foam, add the onions and cinnamon. Cook for 5 minutes or until the bottom of the pan begins to brown. Add the wine, cauliflower, saffron, and bay leaf. Cook until the wine is reduced by two-thirds.

Add the chicken stock and bring to a boil. Reduce heat to a simmer and cook for 15 minutes. Stir in the salt.

Remove from heat and cool slightly. Purée the soup in a high-speed blender. Pass the mixture through a medium strainer. Taste and adjust salt, if necessary, and garnish with the cauliflower florets.

Beet and Apple Cider Soup with Curried Walnuts

1 tbsp (15 mL) unsalted butter
2¼ cups (550 mL) peeled, diced beets
¼ cup (60 mL) diced Spanish onion
½ cup (125 mL) peeled, cored, diced Granny Smith apple
2 cups (500 mL) chicken stock (see page 208)
¾ cup (175 mL) apple cider
1 tbsp (15 mL) cider vinegar
Salt

Curried Walnuts
1 egg white
½ tsp (2 mL) ground cumin
½ tsp (2 mL) ground coriander
½ tsp (2 mL) ground turmeric
½ tsp (2 mL) ground fenugreek
¼ tsp (1 mL) salt
1 tbsp (15 mL) pure maple syrup
8 walnut halves

Beet and Apple Cider Soup
In a large saucepan set over medium heat, heat the butter until it foams; add the beets and onions and cook, covered, until the vegetables are tender, about 10 minutes. Add the apple and continue to cook, covered, for 5 minutes.

Add the chicken stock, apple cider, and cider vinegar; bring to a boil. Reduce heat and simmer for 15 minutes.

Remove from heat. In a blender, purée the soup in batches and season with salt to taste. Pass the mixture through a medium strainer; taste and adjust seasoning if necessary.

Curried Walnuts
Preheat the oven to 325°F (160°C). Beat the egg white until frothy. Whisk in cumin, coriander, turmeric, fenugreek, and salt until well combined. Whisk in maple syrup. Toss with walnuts until well coated. Remove walnuts from egg mixture; shake off excess liquid, and spread walnuts evenly on a parchment paper–lined baking sheet. Bake in preheated oven for 5 minutes. Cool on tray. Break into smaller pieces, if large, before using.

Spiced Pumpkin with Pear Soup

1 tbsp (15 mL) butter
1 tbsp (15 mL) canola oil
1/4 tsp (1 mL) ground cinnamon
1/4 tsp (1 mL) ground coriander
1/4 tsp (1 mL) ground cloves
1/4 tsp (1 mL) ground allspice
2 1/2 cups (625 mL) peeled, seeded, diced
  pumpkin or squash
1/2 cup (125 mL) sliced leek
1 tbsp (15 mL) granulated sugar (optional)
3/4 cup (175 mL) peeled, cored, diced
  Bartlett pear
3 1/2 cups (875 mL) chicken stock (see page
  208)
1/2 tsp (2 mL) vanilla extract
1 tsp (15 mL) minced fresh ginger
3/4 tsp (4 mL) salt or to taste
1/2 tsp (2 mL) cider vinegar or to taste
1 tbsp (15 mL) finely diced pear

Spiced Pumpkin with Pear Soup

In a large saucepan set over medium-high heat,
melt the butter with the oil. Once the butter begins to foam, add the cinnamon, coriander,
cloves, and allspice. Cook the spices for 30 seconds, stirring constantly; add the diced pumpkin
and leek. If using a large, less sweet pumpkin or
squash, add the sugar; otherwise, omit the
sugar and proceed to cook, partially covered, for
20 to 25 minutes or until the pumpkin begins to
break down and brown slightly. Stir in the pear,
scraping the bottom of the pan with a wooden
spoon to loosen any caramelized bits. Cook, stirring, until the pumpkin and pears are mushy.
Add a little of the chicken stock, if necessary, to
prevent scorching.

Stir in the chicken stock and bring to a boil. Reduce heat and simmer for 10 minutes. Add the
vanilla and ginger; cook for 2 minutes and remove from heat.

Purée the soup in a high-speed blender. Season
with salt and vinegar. Pass the mixture through
a medium strainer. Taste and adjust salt and
vinegar if necessary. Garnish each bowl with an
equal amount of diced pear.

Lobster Quiche with Vanilla,
Organic Baby Greens,
and Lemon Vinaigrette

Derek Bendig,

Pangaea's chef de cuisine, is what most people would call a real man. He's a rugged, plain talker who once chased down and beat up a mugger who tried to relieve him of his wallet while Derek was on his way home from work in the wee hours. You look up the word "macho" in the dictionary and it lists his Facebook address as the place to find a living example.

That's why I love that Derek is our quiche master at Pangaea. He's turned the old cliché that real men don't eat quiche completely on its head. Derek not only perfected the recipe for these petite lobster quiches, but he has been known to bring a king-sized lobster quiche to Pangaea staff parties. So if you were hesitating to make or serve this recipe because you thought it might be too feminine, I suggest you reconsider. You really don't want me to send Derek over to help you change your mind.

For 6 servings

Tart Pastry
2 cups (500 mL) all-purpose flour
1 tsp (5 mL) fine salt
1 cup (250 mL) finely cubed cold butter
1/4 cup (60 mL) ice water (approx.)

Filling
1 cup (250 mL) half-and-half (10%) cream
2 tbsp (30 mL) leek, white part only, halved
    and sliced thinly
1 tsp (5 mL) chopped fresh tarragon leaves
1 tsp (5 mL) minced garlic
1 tsp minced shallot
1/2 tsp (2 mL) minced jalapeño pepper
    or jalapeño sauce
1/4 vanilla bean, scraped
Pinch freshly grated nutmeg
2 eggs
1/2 cup (125 mL) parcooked, drained, diced
    lobster meat, about 1 fresh 1 1/4 lb (600 g)
lobster (see page 144 for instructions)
Sea salt and freshly ground black pepper
    to taste

Salad
2 tsp (10 mL) freshly squeezed lemon juice
1/2 vanilla bean or 3 drops pure vanilla extract
1 tsp (5 mL) liquid honey
1/2 tsp (2 mL) grated lemon zest
Pinch salt
Pinch freshly ground pepper
1/2 cup (125 mL) grapeseed oil
12 cups (3 L) organic baby greens

Tart Pastry
In a large bowl, combine the flour and salt until well blended. Cut in the butter until the mixture resembles wet sand. Add in the water, using only as much as you need to form a ball, and mix until the dough just starts to come together. Flatten the ball into a disk. Wrap tightly in plastic wrap and refrigerate for at least 1 hour.

Butter the cups of a 6-cup jumbo muffin tin. Divide the dough into 6 equal portions. Roll each piece into a ball, then roll out thinly on a clean, dry, lightly floured work surface. Use each portion to line a muffin cup, but do not trim or flute tops. Place in the freezer for 1/2 hour to firm up.

Preheat the oven to 400°F (200°C). Blind-bake the shells: Line the inside of the dough cups with parchment paper and fill with dried beans, rice, or small baking weights. Place the muffin tin on the lowest shelf of the oven and bake for 15 minutes. Remove from oven and cool for 5 minutes. Reduce oven temperature to 325°F (160°C). Remove the weights and lining and return the shells to the oven for 10 minutes. Remove from oven and cool for 5 minutes before adding filling.

Filling
In a small saucepan set over medium heat, combine the cream, leek, tarragon, garlic, shallot, jalapeño, vanilla, and nutmeg. Stirring, bring to a boil; immediately remove from heat. In a large bowl, whisk the eggs. Whisking constantly, add a splash of the scalded cream mixture to temper the eggs and blend well. Add the remaining cream mixture and blend well. Cool to room temperature.

Pat the lobster dry and sprinkle an equal amount into each of the prepared pastry shells. Divide the cream mixture evenly over the lobster. Place the pan on the lowest rack in the preheated oven and bake for 30 to 35 minutes or until filling is almost set. Cool on a rack for 15 minutes before removing quiches from pan.

Salad
Place the lemon juice in a small bowl. Scrape the seeds from the inside of the halved vanilla bean pod and add to the lemon juice. Whisk in the honey, lemon zest, salt, and pepper. When blended, whisk in the oil. Drizzle over the greens and toss to coat evenly.

To Assemble
Place a warm or room temperature quiche on each of six serving plates. Divide the salad evenly beside each quiche.

ice wine jelly

With a supple **ice wine jelly** on top, this silken pâté is rich, satisfying, and worth every effort and expense required to make it!

As the essay on page 123 describes, we took a lot of care choosing a foie de canard supplier for Pangaea. In the end, we've created a relationship with a federally inspected supplier for our foie de canard (*foie* is French for "liver," *gras* is French for "fatty," and *canard* is French for "duck," in case you're wondering). Instead of over-feeding their ducks to create mammoth-sized livers, Palmex stops when they grow to about 1 pound (500 g). Not only is this practice more comfortable for the ducks, but it also produces livers with a sumptuous texture.

Even if you're puzzled by the pink salt called for below, don't skip it. Pink salt is sodium nitrite combined with regular salt, and it performs an important preservative function in this and other cured-meat recipes. It is dyed pink in order to avoid being confused with table salt in homes. It helps to maintain the delicate pink colour of the pâté.

For 10 servings

Foie de Canard
1¼ lb (600 g) foie de canard or foie gras
2 cups (500 mL) whole (homogenized) or 2% milk
1 tsp (5 mL) fine sea salt
¼ tsp (1 mL) granulated sugar
¼ tsp (1 mL) finely ground white pepper
¼ tsp (1 mL) pink salt (also called sodium nitrite or Prague powder #1)
¼ cup (60 mL) Niagara ice wine, divided
10 sterilized glass jars, 2 oz (60 mL) each, with wire bail closures
1 tsp (5 mL) gelatin

Apple Compote
1 tsp (5 mL) butter
1 cup (250 mL) peeled, cored, finely diced Gala apple
Pinch ground green or white cardamom seeds
Pinch ground Sri Lankan or other cinnamon
1 sprig fresh thyme

Toasted Rounds
1 loaf multi-grain bread, unsliced
1 tbsp (15 mL) extra virgin olive oil

Foie de canard

Rinse the foie de canard under cold water and pat dry gently. Place in a dish that is narrow and deep enough to allow the meat to be immersed in milk. Add the milk. Cover tightly and refrigerate overnight.

The next day, remove the foie de canard from the milk; discard milk. Rinse meat under cold water. Pat dry and then wrap with a paper towel; let stand at room temperature for 45 minutes or until the foie de canard comes to room temperature. Unwrap and gently pull the lobes apart along the natural separation points. As you work on the first piece, keep the other(s) covered with paper towels.

Remove the membrane that covers the outside of the foie de canard by finding the primary vein on the underside; using your fingers, pull the liver apart along this line into two more pieces. Continue removing any and all detectable veins, breaking the lobe into smaller and smaller pieces while you do so. Use the tip of a wooden skewer to help tease out any hard-to-get-to veins. (When you're done, the foie gras will be in many pieces, some as small as a dime.) Transfer pieces to a bowl.

Blend the sea salt with the sugar, white pepper, and pink salt. Sprinkle evenly over the foie de canard and drizzle over 3 tbsp (45 mL) of the ice wine. Using the tips of your fingers or a small rubber spatula, carefully massage the seasonings into the liver until smooth. Place the foie de canard in a stainless steel bowl that will fit over a saucepan and cover tightly with plastic wrap, pressing the film directly onto the mixture and squeezing out any excess air. Refrigerate overnight.

The next day, fill a saucepan one-third full with water and bring to a simmer. Once the water simmers, remove the foie de canard from the refrigerator and place the bowl over the saucepan. Gently stir the foie gras with a rubber spatula until it liquefies and is just warm to the touch, 105°F (40°C) on an instant-read thermometer. Remove the bowl from the heat and continue stirring until the mixture cools slightly.

Pass the mixture through a fine-mesh chinois or tamis (drum) sieve into a clean glass or stainless-steel container. Press the thick liquid through the holes using a rubber spatula or the bowl of a 2-oz (60 mL) ladle. Transfer this mixture to a piping bag and fill each dry sterilized glass jar two-thirds full. Gently but firmly tap each jar on a cloth-covered counter to remove any air bubbles. Place the jars on a tray and transfer, uncovered, to the refrigerator. (If covered, condensation will form on the inside of the glass, which will be problematic when adding the ice wine gelatin topping.)

Stir the remaining 1 tbsp (15 mL) of ice wine with ¼ cup (60 mL) of cold water. Sprinkle the gelatin over the mixture and gently stir until well combined. Let stand for 10 minutes. Heat this ice wine mixture gently over simmering water until the gelatin granules are dissolved. Refrigerate the mixture until it just begins to thicken, about 5 to 6 minutes.

Pour an equal amount of the gelatin mixture over each jar of foie de canard pâté. Chill for 10 minutes. Cover tightly and let stand in the refrigerator for at least 24 hours.

Foie de Canard in a Bottle, with Apple Compote and Toasted Rounds

Apple Compote

In a small skillet set over medium-high heat, melt the butter. Blend the apple with the cardamom and cinnamon; toss in the sprig of thyme and add to the skillet. Cook, stirring gently, for 6 to 7 minutes or until the edges of the diced apple begin to soften but not break down. Remove from heat and cool to room temperature. Remove and discard the thyme sprig and refrigerate compote.

Toasted Rounds

Preheat oven to 275°F (140°C). Slice the multi-grain loaf into very thin slices. Using a 2-inch (5 cm) round cookie cutter, stamp out small rounds and place on a metal rimmed baking sheet. Drizzle with olive oil and bake in preheated oven for 5 to 6 minutes or until rounds begin to brown. Remove from oven and reserve at room temperature until needed.

To Assemble

Open a container of the pâté and place on a serving plate. Garnish with equal amounts of the compote and a few toast rounds.

Pan-Seared Foie de Canard
on French Toast with Peach Compote

Ace Bakery

opened in 1993, starting a new movement in Toronto. Suddenly, it was possible for even small restaurants to offer an interesting breadbasket stocked with handmade European-style rustic breads. I've been a fan of theirs since the beginning, and their fine wares are served in Pangaea breadbaskets, too.

One of Ace Bakery's star offerings is pain au lait, slightly sweet mini loaves with a soft crust and a delicate but rich crumb. I use them in this recipe to make two bite-sized pieces of French toast to accompany seared foie de canard. I find that the egg in the French-toast mixture extends the flavour of the foie gras because egg is a neutral foil for other rich flavours. If you can't get pain au lait, substitute brioche or trimmed challah slices.

For 8 servings

Peach Compote
1 cup (250 mL) granulated sugar
1 cup (250 mL) water
1/2 vanilla bean, scraped
4 peaches

French Toast
4 pain au lait mini loaves
1 cup (250 mL) half-and-half (10%) cream
2 eggs, beaten
1/4 tsp (1 mL) salt
Pinch freshly grated nutmeg
2 tbsp (30 mL) butter

Foie de Canard
1 1/4 lbs (600 g) whole foie de canard lobe
1/2 tsp (2 mL) salt
Freshly ground black pepper

Peach Compote

Combine the sugar and water in a saucepan. Bring to a boil. Add the vanilla bean and set aside.

Slice an X in the skin at the bottom of each peach and place in a metal bowl. Pour boiling water into the bowl and let stand for 30 seconds. Drain and cover peaches with ice water. Let peaches stand for 5 minutes. Slip the skins off the peaches and pat dry. Halve each peach by slicing around the pit; twist apart. Remove the pits and place the peach halves in the saucepan with the simple syrup and vanilla; bring to a boil. Reduce the heat and simmer for 15 minutes. Remove from heat and allow peaches to cool in syrup.

French Toast

Slice the long sides from each pain au lait mini loaf to make a rectangular piece of bread. Discard trimmings. Slice each loaf in half lengthwise.

In a shallow bowl, combine the cream, eggs, salt, and nutmeg. Beat until smooth. Submerge the bread in this mixture, working in batches if necessary, and soak for 3 to 4 minutes.

In a large non-stick skillet set over medium heat, melt the butter. Shake off any residual egg mixture from the bread and add to pan. Cook for 2 minutes and turn; repeat three times (total cooking time will be 8 minutes) until French toast is golden all over and dry to the touch. Keep warm. (If you have two ovens, preheat one to 140°F (60°C) and transfer cooked toasts to it while you prepare the foie de canard.)

Foie de Canard

Preheat oven to 350°F (180°C). Position the lobe of foie de canard horizontally so the tapered ends are on your left and right on a cutting board. Slice the liver into 8 slices, 2 1/2 oz (75 g) each. The slices on the outer ends will be thicker than the inner slices.

Preheat a dry cast-iron pan over medium heat for 45 to 60 seconds. Sear the foie de canard for 1 1/2 minutes per side, adding an additional 30 seconds per side to the cooking time for the thicker end pieces.

Transfer to a baking sheet and let rest at room temperature for 2 minutes. Then roast in the preheated oven for 5 minutes or until each piece is firm but still yields easily when touched with your fingertip. Season both sides with salt and pepper.

To Assemble

Place a piece of French toast on a plate. Slice each piece of peach three or four times all the way through and fan slices in a straight line over top of French toast. Place a piece of seared foie de canard on top of peaches. Spoon any juices that accumulated while cooking and resting the foie de canard evenly over each dish.

Bone Marrow
with Celeriac and Parsley Salad

Roasted

bone marrow. I'm not sure how far back this dish dates — it's certainly a bistro classic — but I think it must have originated in prehistory, when every single speck of food was mined for its full nutritional value. Regardless, bone marrow served with a tart, palate-cleansing salad is a popular snack at our bar; it's a perfect after-work or pre-theatre nibble since it satisfies hunger pangs nicely.

By the way, if the term "ficelle" is unfamiliar to you, it's a thin version of a baguette and is about the thickness of a bread stick. We have ficelles delivered twice a day so they're super fresh at both lunch and dinner.

For 6 servings

6 veal thigh bones, each 2¹/₂ inches
    (6 cm) long
¹/₂ tsp (2 mL) salt
Freshly ground black pepper
¹/₄ celeriac, peeled
¹/₂ cup (125 mL) lightly packed Italian
    parsley leaves
1 tsp (5 mL) freshly squeezed lemon juice
2 tbsp (30 mL) olive oil
36 thin slices ficelle or 6 slices French bread,
    grilled or toasted
Sea salt and freshly cracked black pepper

Preheat oven to 375°F (190°C). Stand the marrow bones upright on a rimmed baking sheet and bake in the preheated oven for 15 minutes. Remove and keep at room temperature.

Just before serving, return the bones to the preheated oven for 5 minutes. Remove and sprinkle the top of the marrow with salt and pepper.

Meanwhile, slice the celeriac thinly and cut into wedges, each about the same size as a parsley leaf. Toss with the parsley, lemon juice, and oil.

To Assemble

On an oblong plate, stand one marrow bone, thickest end down, at one end. Add a small amount of salad in the middle and stack the bread slices at the other end.

Pear and Endive Salad
with Shaved Fennel, Watercress,
Frisée, Walnuts, Tiger Blue Cheese,
and Mustard Dressing

Roquefort

and Stilton are famous European cheeses that for many people will always be the benchmarks that define greatness in the blue cheese category. But others realize that Canada has mastered the art of making blue cheese, too. In fact, there is no doubt to me that our blue cheeses can compete on an international level. In this signature salad, I use a British Columbian blue cheese called Tiger Blue. It has a terrific balance, offering sweetness, creamy texture, and pungency that complement roasted pears and walnuts perfectly.

For 6 servings

Roasted Pears
3 Bosc or other firm pear
1 tsp (5 mL) canola oil

Toasted Walnuts
1/3 cup (75 mL) California walnut pieces

Pear Crisps
1/4 cup (60 mL) granulated sugar
1/4 cup (60 mL) water
1 Bosc or other firm pear

Fennel
1 small bulb fennel
1 1/2 tsp (7 mL) pickling spice
1 cup (250 mL) water
1/2 cup (125 mL) white wine vinegar
1/2 cup (125 mL) granulated sugar
1/4 tsp (1 mL) salt

Mustard Dressing
3 tbsp (45 mL) Dijon mustard
3 tbsp (45 mL) vegetable oil
2 tsp (10 mL) red wine vinegar
2 tsp (10 mL) liquid honey
2 tsp (10 mL) finely chopped shallot
1/2 tsp (2 mL) salt
1/2 tsp (2 mL) freshly ground white pepper

Salad
1 head frisée, trimmed, washed, and dried
2 bunches organic or hydroponic watercress, about 2 cups (500 mL) lightly packed
3 oz (90 g) Tiger Blue or other blue cheese, such as Stilton

Roasted Pears
Preheat the oven to 350°F (180°C). Cut the pears in half lengthwise. With a melon baller, remove the cores of the pears and brush the cut sides with oil. Place the pear halves, cut-side up, on a rimmed baking sheet. Bake for 25 minutes; rotate tray and bake for 10 minutes longer. Remove from oven and reserve for up to 4 hours.

Toasted Walnuts
Blanch the walnut pieces in salted water for 3 minutes and drain. Spread them out on a parchment paper–lined, rimmed metal baking sheet and bake at 350°F (180°C) for 10 minutes, until dry and crunchy but not coloured.

Pear Crisps
Combine the sugar and water in a saucepan set over high heat. Bring to a boil and simmer, without stirring, until the mixture is crystal clear. Cool to room temperature.

Meanwhile, reduce the oven to 200°F (100°C) and use a mandoline to slice the remaining pear into slices about the thickness of a dime. Brush with cooled syrup mixture on each side. Spread slices out on a silicone- or parchment paper–lined baking sheet. Bake for 10 minutes or for up to 25 minutes, until very crisp. Cool on a rack before carefully transferring to an airtight container.

Fennel
Trim the root end and tops from the fennel. Using a mandoline, slice the fennel into paper-thin ribbons.

Tie the pickling spices in a cheesecloth bundle and place in a saucepan; add the water, vinegar, sugar, and salt. Bring to a boil; reduce the heat and simmer for 5 minutes. Add the fennel and return to a boil. Remove from heat and allow the fennel to cool in the liquid. Remove the pickling spice sachet and discard. Store the cooled fennel in its cooking juices in the refrigerator for up to 3 days.

Mustard Dressing
In a bowl, whisk together the mustard, oil, vinegar, honey, shallot, salt, and white pepper until well combined. Refrigerate for 2 hours. Strain and refrigerate for up to 2 days.

To Assemble
Tear the frisée into bite-sized tufts. Remove the fennel from the pickling juices, drain, and toss with frisée. Drizzle with enough dressing to lightly coat salad and toss well.

Divide frisée mixture among six plates. Lean a bouquet of watercress against each mound of frisée. Stand both a pear chip and a roasted pear half against the watercress. Garnish with cheese and walnuts. Drizzle additional dressing around the salad.

Lobster Risotto

Marcella Hazen,

the great Italian chef, was interviewed by my wife, Dana McCauley, for *The Toronto Sun*. The interview took place at Pangaea, and afterward Marcella and I stepped into the kitchen to whip up a few dishes for the newspaper's cameraman. I loved her! She was confident to the point of being crusty but also very right that making seafood risotto with water produces the cleanest flavour and allows the seafood to really sing. Although I break a cardinal rule of Italian cooking that stipulates that you never pair Parmesan with fish, my customers tell me this is the best lobster risotto they've ever tasted!

Now a word about lobster. As noted elsewhere in these pages, I prefer to use locally sourced products whenever possible. Although I think Canadian lobsters from the icy Canadian Atlantic waters are superior-tasting and one of the purest products available, at Pangaea I use Massachusetts lobster, which are recommended by Ocean Wise. (The argument against Canadian lobsters is that the harvesting equipment can entangle and harm whales like humpbacks and sperm whales, as well as North Atlantic right whales, which are the most critically endangered species on the planet.) As I write this, Nova Scotia is reviewing its catchers' lobster harvesting practices, and I'm hopeful that the changes the province is proposing will allow me to purchase their fine seafood very soon.

For 4 servings

Lobster

¹⁄₄ cup (60 mL) vegetable oil
1 cup (250 mL) coarsely chopped carrots
1 cup (250 mL) coarsely chopped celery
1 cup (250 mL) coarsely chopped Spanish onion
1 tbsp (15 mL) whole black peppercorns
2 bay leaves
2 cloves garlic, halved
³⁄₄ cup (175 mL) salt or to taste
2 Atlantic lobsters, each 1¹⁄₄ lbs (600 g)
1 cup (250 mL) butter sauce (see page 213)

Risotto

5 tbsp (75 mL) butter, divided
2 tbsp (30 mL) canola oil
¹⁄₄ cup (50 mL) finely diced Spanish onion
1 cup (250 mL) Superfino Arborio or
    Carnaroli rice
1 bay leaf
¹⁄₂ cup (125 mL) dry white wine
8 cups (2 L) simmering water
¹⁄₂ cup (125 mL) washed and thinly sliced leeks
2 cloves garlic, minced
¹⁄₄ tsp (1 mL) minced jalapeño pepper or
    jalapeño sauce
¹⁄₄ cup (50 mL) freshly grated Parmesan cheese
2 tbsp (30 mL) extra virgin olive oil (approx.)
1 cup (250 mL) grape tomatoes
¹⁄₄ cup (50 mL) chopped fresh parsley leaves
Salt and freshly ground black pepper

Lobster

Heat the vegetable oil in a large stockpot set over medium-high heat. When the oil is hot, add the carrots, celery, and onion. When the vegetables begin to sizzle, stir well and cover pot; cook for 2 minutes. Stir in the peppercorns, bay leaves, and garlic. Fill the pot with 32 cups (8 L) water or enough to come to 2 inches (5 cm) from the top of the stockpot. Cover and bring to a boil. Remove the lid and add the salt.

Remove the elastic bands from the lobster claws. Plunge both lobsters head first into the boiling water and cook for 6 minutes. Remove the lobsters from the boiling water using tongs and plunge them directly into an ice bath. Let stand in ice water for 15 minutes. Drain well and pat dry.

To clean the lobster: Firmly grasp the tail and twist a quarter-turn to separate it from the body. Place the tip of a heavy knife at the base of the tail and press the blade down to divide the tail in half lengthwise. Remove the meat from the shell.

Remove the arms and claws from the body. Separate the claws from the arms. Balance the claw on its side with the pincher facing up. With the heel of your knife, carefully but purposefully strike the claw with a sharp hit that lands ¹⁄₂ inch (1 cm) behind the pincher; twist the blade to crack the shell of the claw in half. Remove the loose shell and then clasp the pincher; jiggle it from side to side until you can pull away the shell and leave the meat attached to the claw. Clasp the back of the lobster claw and remove the meat from the shell. Lay the lobster claw meat on its side and remove the centre cartilage. Repeat for the other claw. With a pair of kitchen shears, cut the shell of the lobster arms lengthwise and remove the meat. You should have 2 cups/500 mL in all.

Place all the meat in a small saucepan; add the butter sauce and keep warm, but do not boil.

Risotto

In a large, heavy-bottomed saucepan set over medium-high heat, melt 1 tbsp (15 mL) of the butter with the oil. When the butter begins to foam, add the onion and sauté for 2 to 3 minutes or until soft and translucent. Add the rice and sauté, stirring and scraping the bottom with a wooden spoon continuously, until the rice begins to toast and the edges become slightly translucent.

Stir in the bay leaf and white wine and wait for the first bubbles to appear around the edge of the pan. Begin adding the simmering water, 1 cup (250 mL) at a time. Between each addition of water, stir the mixture with a wooden spoon for 2 to 4 minutes or until the water is almost completely absorbed. Repeat this step until all but the last ¹⁄₂ cup (125 mL)

of water is used (this process should take approximately 20 minutes). Add this water, the leeks, and the garlic; using the wooden spoon, work the risotto hard with the back of the spoon during the last few minutes of cooking.

Stir in the jalapeño, Parmesan, extra virgin olive oil, and remaining butter. Add the grape tomatoes, parsley, and lobster meat. Cook, stirring, until heated through, about 2 minutes. Season to taste with salt and pepper and serve immediately with a little extra virgin olive oil drizzled on top.

Tips
Save the lobster shells for making bisque another day.

If you prefer, you can buy fresh, cooked, shelled lobster at the fish market. Purchase 2 cups (500 mL) for this recipe.

Roasted Roulade of Duck Breast
with Napa Cabbage, Apple,
and Wild Ontario Pine Mushrooms

Duck

Duck roulade is a recipe I'm proud of creating. Although I'm far from a Luddite, I get great pleasure from cooking as if it's 1922.

At Pangaea, we have immersion thermo circulators that we use to cook many foods "sous vide," and I'm fascinated by the wonderful results they produce. That said, I was very gratified when I made this dish for the 2008 Grand Cru luncheon that raises money for Toronto Western Hospital. I was paired with New York restaurateur Daniel Boulud to create a $12,500-a-plate lunch that would complement vintage Château Le Pin wines.

We were presenting the lunch together, but Daniel's team and mine were taking turns making courses. When he saw this duck being plated, he couldn't resist tasting it and complimenting me on the flavour and texture and how well I'd used "sous vide." When I told him I'd cooked the duck the old-fashioned way, he called his cooks over to see how we had used traditional tools and my signature roasting method to make a perfect product. It was great to have a chef I respect recognize our team's skill! (Another big fan of this dish is my son, Oliver. In fact, the tell-all book he'll write later in life will likely be called *Tales of a Teenage Duck-a-holic*.)

The great news is that you can have the exact same results by following this recipe. You'll see that the meat is rested twice during cooking, and this is the step that ensures that the duck is perfectly and evenly cooked.

For 6 servings

Duck Roulades

3 large Muscovy or Mullard duck breasts, about 1 lb (500 g) each
Salt
Freshly ground black pepper
1 tbsp (15 mL) canola oil
1/2 cup (125 mL) dark chicken reduction (see page 209)

Napa Cabbage

1 head (2 lb/1 kg or 10 cups/1250 mL julienned) Napa cabbage
1 tbsp (15 mL) canola oil
2 cups (500 mL) thinly sliced onion
1 cup (250 mL) bacon lardons (see tip page 149), about 6 oz (180 g)
1 tsp (5 mL) minced garlic
1 cup (250 mL) white wine
1 small Gala apple, cored and diced to make 1/2 cup (125 mL)
1/2 cup (125 mL) whipping (35%) cream
1/4 cup (60 mL) dark chicken reduction (see page 209)
1/4 tsp (1 mL) freshly grated nutmeg
1 tsp (5 mL) salt or to taste
1/4 tsp (1 mL) finely ground white pepper or to taste

Mushrooms

1 tbsp (15 mL) butter
2 cups (500 mL) trimmed wild Ontario pine or porcini mushrooms
1 tsp (5 mL) white wine
1/4 tsp (1 mL) freshly squeezed lemon juice
1/4 tsp (1 mL) salt or to taste

Duck Roulades

Lay the duck breasts skin-side down and use a sharp knife to trim away any sinew and silver skin or fat on the meaty side. Loosen the tenderloin using your fingers and slice it off the breast (reserve for another use).

Using a sharp knife, partially remove the fat cap from each duck breast so it still hinges along one side of the duck breast like the cover of a book: Begin prying the fat cap up by inserting your fingertips between the fat and muscle; continue to separate the fat from the meat until it is no longer easy to do so. Then use the tip of a long, thin knife with a flexible blade to separate the fat until it's just attached along the long edge opposite where you started.

Pat the hinged meat and skin flat. Lay your knife flat, parallel to the length of the breast, and slice to butterfly the meaty side so that it opens like a flap on a book cover. Pat flat. (If the skin and fat layer is very thick, butterfly as well to create a fourth flap.)

Season the duck meat all over with salt and pepper. Beginning at the short, meaty end, start rolling the meat tightly until the fat is snugly rolled around the meat. Truss the ducks snugly at 1/2-inch (1 cm) intervals with butcher's twine; the trusses should be slack enough to allow the meat to expand as it cooks. (Duck can be prepared to this point, wrapped well, and refrigerated for up to 3 days.)

Napa Cabbage

Julienne the cabbage leaves. In a Dutch oven set over medium-high, heat the oil. Add the onion and bacon and fry until the onion is tender and the bacon begins to colour slightly. Lower the heat to medium and stir in the cabbage and garlic; cook, uncovered, for 5 minutes, stirring well. Add the white wine and simmer for 5 minutes or until the wine is reduced by about two-thirds. Add the diced apple and cream; simmer for 10 minutes to reduce by half or until the liquid coats the back of a spoon. Add duck reduction and simmer for 5 minutes. Add nutmeg and season with salt and white pepper to taste. Keep warm until the duck is ready.

Mushrooms

In a skillet set over medium-high heat, melt the butter until it starts to foam. Add the mushrooms and sauté until golden. Add the wine and lemon juice and season with salt to taste. Reserve.

To Assemble

Pat the duck roulades dry and season the exteriors lightly with salt and pepper. Heat the oil in a skillet set over medium-high heat. When the oil is hot, sear each roulade on all sides until golden. Arrange the browned duck on a rack set over a rimmed baking sheet and let rest for 20 minutes. Meanwhile, preheat the oven to 375°F (190°C). Roast for 10 minutes. Remove and rest for 8 minutes, turning once before cutting.

Meanwhile, heat the remaining ¹/₂ cup (125 mL) reduction. Cut and remove the twine from around the duck. Spoon a little sauce in the middle of six large, round plates. Place a mound of the Napa cabbage mixture in the centre of the sauce. Cut the duck into thin medallions and place 3 medallions around the cabbage. Scatter the mushrooms over the top of the cabbage, letting them fall where they may.

Tip

A lardon is a strip of bacon about ³/₄ inch (2 cm) long and ¹/₈ inch (3 mm) thick.

Pine mushrooms *(Tricholoma magnivelare)*, also called American matsutake mushrooms, are elusive fungi. While some people look for them poking up through the forest floor, others swear they can find them by smell! Angela Houpt, our mushroom forager, says she most often finds these autumn mushrooms growing under fallen pine needles and leaves. Pine mushrooms have a symbiotic relationship with their environment; they need to be picked sparingly so there are always some left to fruit the next crop.

While **home-testing** the recipes for this book, I realized one of the reasons people come to Pangaea: Re-creating my recipes at home means using a lot of pots and pans!

At Pangaea, caribou is on the menu only when in season. The Inuit caribou hunt takes place in Nunavut each August and September, and we buy some of this meat. The hunt is the largest in the world, providing a major source of employment for the Inuit of Rankin Inlet and Coral Harbour, and affects the area's GDP significantly.

For 4 servings

Caribou

1½ lbs (750 g) piece caribou strip loin roast
1 tbsp (15 mL) juniper berries, coarsely crushed
½ cup (125 mL) chopped fresh Italian parsley
3 cloves garlic, chopped
1 tbsp (15 mL) black peppercorns, crushed
3 tbsp (45 mL) canola oil, divided
½ tsp (2 mL) salt
½ tsp (2 mL) freshly ground pepper
⅔ cup (150 mL) veal reduction (see page 210)

Lemon-Thyme Spätzle

3 eggs
¼ cup (60 mL) half-and-half (10%) cream
1 tbsp (15 mL) chopped thyme or lemon thyme leaves
½ tsp (2 mL) salt
¼ tsp (1 mL) freshly ground white pepper or to taste
Finely grated zest of 1 lemon
1⅓ cups (325 mL) all-purpose flour
1 tbsp (15 mL) butter
1 tbsp (15 mL) canola oil

Vegetables

½ lb (250 g) fresh or rehydrated dried chestnuts
½ lb (250 g) maple-cured slab bacon
1 tbsp (15 mL) butter
¼ cup (60 mL) julienne strips white onion
1 tbsp (15 mL) pure maple syrup
2 tbsp (30 mL) veal reduction (see page 210)
Salt and freshly ground black pepper to taste

Because caribou is such a lean meat, it's best cooked to no more than medium-rare, but I recommend that you serve it rare to retain maximum flavour, texture, and tenderness. In fact, if you serve caribou well done, chances are no one will eat it, since it tends to get quite tough and develop a strong, livery flavour.

This recipe also calls for juniper berries, which are native to North America and plentiful in Canada. While their hallmark flavouring is often associated with gin, juniper berries will impart only a subtle, menthol-tinged pungency to meats like caribou — so try it; you'll like it.

Caribou

Trim away any excess fat or gristle and cut the caribou crosswise into 4 medallions of equal thickness. Combine the juniper berries, parsley, garlic, peppercorns, and 2 tbsp (30 mL) of the oil in a large bowl. Pat the caribou dry and coat each piece of meat with the marinade; cover and refrigerate for at least 30 minutes or for up to 6 hours.

Preheat the oven to 325°F (160°C). Set an ovenproof skillet over medium-high heat and add the remaining oil. Remove caribou from the marinade and shake off any excess. Season with salt and pepper and sear all sides evenly; let rest for 10 minutes. Transfer the skillet to the oven and roast for 8 to 10 minutes; remove and let the meat rest on a cutting board in a warm area for 10 minutes. (This resting period before and after cooking allows the internal temperature to rise and the juices inside to recirculate, giving the meat a more uniform degree of doneness.)

Lemon-Thyme Spätzle

In a large mixing bowl, combine the eggs, cream, thyme, salt, white pepper, and lemon zest. Gradually add the flour until a thick, glutinous dough develops. Using an electric stand mixer fitted with a paddle attachment, beat on medium speed until smooth and elastic; scrape down the sides of the bowl as necessary. Cover and let rest in the refrigerator for 1 hour.

Place a Dutch oven filled with lightly salted water over high heat; bring to a boil. Measuring out a cupful (250 mL) at a time, place some spätzle dough on one end of a small, smooth cutting board. Orient the board so that the spätzle dough is at the far end of the board from the mouth of the boiling stockpot. Dip a pallet knife into the boiling water and run it down the bare length of the cutting board to moisten it evenly. (This will prevent the sticky batter from adhering to the board.)

Spread the batter into a ¼-inch (6 mm) thick sheet. Using the palette knife, scrape long, thin ribbons of batter into the pot of rapidly boiling salted water. Return to a boil and cook for 1 minute. Remove cooked spätzle with a slotted spoon; transfer to a lightly oiled pan to cool. Repeat, working in small batches, allowing the water to return to a boil between each batch.

Vegetables

If using fresh chestnuts, prevent them from exploding in the oven by cutting a slit in the top of each shell using the tip of a very sharp paring knife. Preheat the oven to 400°F (200°C), place the chestnuts in an ovenproof pan, and roast for 15 to 20 minutes, tossing occasionally. When cool enough to handle, peel away the shells and rub away the paper-thin membrane surrounding the nutmeats using a clean kitchen towel. Use the tip of a small paring knife or a wooden skewer to

Roasted Caribou with Lemon-Thyme Spätzle, Chestnuts, and Maple-Cured Bacon

clean out the nooks and crannies. Dice the chestnuts. If using dried chestnuts, rehydrate by soaking in simmering water for 30 minutes before dicing.

If necessary, remove the skin from the slab bacon. Slice the bacon into ¼-inch (6 mm) thick slices and then dice. In a small skillet set over medium-high heat, melt the butter. When the butter foams, add the onions and sauté until soft. Add the bacon and continue to sauté until caramelized.

Drain off the fat and add the reserved chestnuts, maple syrup, and veal reduction. Bring to a boil. Season to taste and keep warm.

To Assemble
Heat the remaining ⅔ cup (150 mL) veal reduction in a small saucepan. Pour in any of the juices that accumulated on the cutting board while the caribou was resting.

In yet another skillet, heat the butter and oil called for in the spätzle recipe. Sauté spätzle until the edges are golden. Taste and adjust the seasoning if necessary.

Place a small portion of spätzle in the centre of four heated plates. Surround the spätzle with the onion-bacon-chestnut mixture. Slice the caribou across the grain and place on top of the spätzle. Spoon equal amounts of the veal reduction around each portion.

Peter

Geary, my business partner, and I met when we worked together at Jump Café & Bar in Toronto's financial district. Meeting Peter wasn't the only good thing that happened to me there. I made other great friends while working at Jump, including Michael Bonacini, who is co-owner of that great restaurant still.

Until working with Michael, I'd always found gnocchi to be disappointing, starchy little lumps. The appeal was completely lost on me. Then, while we were developing the first menu for Jump, Michael shared his gnocchi recipe with me. The soft, pillowy little morsels he made were a revelation. I still use the lessons I learned from him that day each time I make gnocchi myself.

So I dedicate this recipe to Michael, who is equal parts Italian and Welsh. While cheese melted with beer wouldn't be delicious drizzled over gnocchi, I used an auditory play on words to create this dish, which features Italian potato dumplings sauced with rabbit, which sounds like "rarebit," which in turn is Welsh. Get it? (Yeah, I know; if you have to explain a joke, it doesn't really work, does it?)

For 6 servings

Gnocchi
1 tub (8 oz/250 g) ricotta cheese
3/4 cup (175 mL) all-purpose flour (approx.)
1 egg
1 cup (250 mL) mashed or riced cooked russet potato
1 cup (250 mL) chopped fresh parsley
2 cloves roasted garlic (see page 212), puréed
1/4 tsp (1 mL) salt
1/4 tsp (1 mL) freshly ground black pepper
1/4 tsp (1 mL) freshly grated nutmeg
1/2 cup (125 mL) cornmeal
1 tbsp (15 mL) butter

Rabbit Ragoût
2 rabbit legs
1 tbsp (15 mL) canola oil (approx.)
1/4 cup (60 mL) diced carrots
1/4 cup (60 mL) diced celery
1/4 cup (60 mL) diced onion
1 tsp (5 mL) chopped garlic
1 bay leaf
1/2 tsp (2 mL) whole black peppercorns
1/2 cup (125 mL) red wine
2 tbsp (30 mL) fresh sage (or 1 tsp dried)
1/4 tsp (1 mL) salt
4 cups (1 L) rabbit stock (approx.) (see page 209)
1/2 cup (125 mL) finely diced, peeled, seeded tomatoes

Squash
1 tbsp (15 mL) canola oil (approx.)
2 cups (500 mL) diced, peeled, seeded butternut squash
1/3 cup (75 mL) diced onion
1 tsp (5 mL) chopped fresh sage leaves
1/4 tsp (1 mL) salt
Parmesan cheese shards

Gnocchi
Place the ricotta cheese in a cheesecloth-lined strainer set over a bowl. Cover and refrigerate for 12 hours or overnight. Discard any accumulated liquid.

Place the drained ricotta cheese in a large bowl. Make a well in the centre; sprinkle over the flour. Crack the egg directly into the bowl. Add the potato, parsley, garlic, salt, pepper, and nutmeg. Mix thoroughly with a spatula or wooden spoon until the mixture starts to form a dough. (If you find the mixture is too wet, adjust by sprinkling with flour and blending well. Or if the mixture is a little too dry, add a little milk or cream. When the dough starts to come away from the bowl and form a ball, the texture is correct.) Coat the dough lightly with flour; cover and let rest in a cool place for 20 minutes.

Dust a large, clean work surface with a little flour; cut the dough into two equal parts and roll into long, ropey lengths, each about the width of a sausage. Using a palate knife, cut the gnocchi into bite-sized pieces. Dust each piece with cornmeal. Transfer to a baking sheet and chill for 1 hour.

Rabbit Ragoût
Rinse the rabbit legs and pat dry. Add the oil to a large saucepan set over medium heat. When hot, sear the rabbit legs for 2 minutes per side or until golden brown. Transfer the legs to a platter and add the carrot, celery, and onions to the hot pan; sauté for 5 minutes, adding additional oil if necessary. Add the garlic, bay leaf, and peppercorns and continue to sauté for 4 minutes or until the vegetables are softened and slightly browned. Add the red wine and simmer for 3 to 4 minutes or until the liquid is reduced by half.

Return the rabbit legs to the pan; stir in the sage and salt. Pour in the rabbit stock. Bring to a boil. Reduce the heat, cover pot, and simmer for 1 hour. Add more stock if necessary to keep legs covered at all times throughout cooking.

When the rabbit is fork tender, remove the legs. Strain the cooking liquid into a clean saucepan. Reduce the cooking liquid for 20 minutes or until thick enough to coat the back of a spoon lightly. Meanwhile, remove the meat from the rabbit legs and shred into bite-sized pieces. Discard the bones. Strain the reduced cooking liquid through a fine sieve. Combine the meat and sauce and cool to room temperature. Refrigerate until needed.

Squash
Heat the oil in a hot skillet set over medium heat. When the oil is hot, add the squash and sauté until well browned on all sides. Add the onions and sauté until squash is tender, adding a little more oil, if necessary, to prevent sticking. Stir in the sage and season to taste. Keep warm until ready to serve.

Potato Gnocchi
with Roasted Garlic and Ricotta Cheese, with Ragoût of Rabbit and Squash

To Assemble

When ready to serve, stir the tomatoes into the ragoût and reheat just until very hot.

In a large pot of boiling salted water, cook the gnocchi in batches for approximately 3 to 4 minutes or until they begin to float and are no longer doughy in the centre. Using a slotted spoon, remove the gnocchi from the boiling water and drain well.

In a non-stick skillet set over medium-high heat, melt the butter until it foams. Add the gnocchi and sauté until golden brown.

Divide the ragoût meat equally among six heated bowls. Arrange the gnocchi around the outside of the rabbit; spoon squash over top. Garnish with Parmesan cheese.

Canadian

cooking is epitomized by this dish: farm-raised Ontario pheasants, candy cane beets from Cookstown Greens, Brussels sprouts from the greenbelt, and wild rice from the lakes of Manitoba.

While most people are familiar with Brussels sprouts, not everyone realizes that they grow in clusters on a long stalk and not out of the ground on single stalks like cabbages. I like to buy Brussels sprouts on their stalks so that they are as fresh as possible — once removed from their stalks, the natural sugars in the sprouts start to convert into starch and the flavour becomes stronger and more pungent.

While game meats can often be assertive and a bit risky as a dinner party choice, pheasant is a mild, light-coloured meat with mass appeal. If pheasants aren't available, substitute chicken breasts and cook until the juices run completely clear.

For 6 servings

Thyme Sauce
1 tbsp (15 mL) unsalted butter
2 tbsp (30 mL) chopped shallots
1/2 tsp (2 mL) coarsely ground black pepper
    or to taste
1 bay leaf
1 clove garlic, minced
1 cup (250 mL) red wine
5 cups (1.25 L) dark chicken stock
    (see page 208)
1/2 tsp (2 mL) finely chopped fresh thyme
    leaves
Salt
1 tsp (5 mL) cold, chopped butter

Pheasant
6 pheasant breasts, 7 oz (210 g) each
2 tbsp (30 mL) thinly sliced garlic
3 tbsp (45 mL) canola oil, divided
1 tsp (5 mL) salt
1/2 tsp (2 mL) freshly ground black pepper

Wild Rice
1 tbsp (15 mL) butter
1/3 cup (75 mL) diced white onion
1 cup (250 mL) wild rice
2 cups (500 mL) chicken stock (see page 208)
1/2 tsp (2 mL) kosher salt

Brussels Sprouts
24 Brussels sprouts, about 1 1/2 lbs (750 g)
1 tbsp (15 mL) butter
1/3 cup (75 mL) minced shallots
Pinch salt
Pinch freshly ground white pepper

Candy Cane Beets
12 baby candy cane beets
1 tbsp (15 mL) butter
Salt and pepper to taste

Thyme Sauce

In a large saucepan set over medium-high heat, melt the butter until it begins to foam. Add the chopped shallots, pepper, and bay leaf. Sauté for 1 minute or until the shallots are golden. Stir in the garlic and cook for 30 seconds.

Deglaze the pan with the red wine, stirring well. Reduce the heat and simmer for 20 minutes or until the liquid is reduced by about half. Add the chicken stock; bring to a boil. Reduce the heat to low and simmer, skimming off and discarding any foam that develops on the top, for 2 hours or until the sauce is thick enough to coat the back of a spoon.

Strain through a fine sieve, pressing the solids down with the round side of a ladle or spoon to remove all the fluid. Stir the thyme into the sauce; taste and season with salt and additional pepper if necessary. (Sauce can be made to this point up to 3 days ahead and reheated just before use.) Reheat the sauce until hot; remove from heat and whisk in the bits of butter. Makes 1/3 cup (75 mL).

Pheasant

"French" the wing bone by removing the tip and then cutting around the base of the joint on the drumette with a small, sharp knife; scrape the meat down the bone toward the breast to expose and clean the bone tip. Blot the meat dry between paper towels. Place pheasant skin-side up on a flat tray. Toss the garlic with 1 tbsp (15 mL) of oil and sprinkle evenly over the pheasant. Cover and refrigerate for 1 hour.

Wild Rice

In a saucepan set over medium heat, melt the butter until it foams; add the onion and cook for 2 minutes or until softened. Add the wild rice, stock, and salt; bring to a boil. Reduce the heat; cover and simmer for 55 to 60 minutes or until the grains are tender and all the liquid has been absorbed. Remove from heat. Taste and add more salt if necessary. Cover and keep warm. (If you're making this component of the meal ahead of time, reheat in a skillet, adding a bit of chicken stock or water to prevent sticking.)

Brussels Sprouts

Fill a Dutch oven or pasta pot three-quarters full with salted water and bring to a boil. Trim away the loose outer leaves of the Brussels sprouts and trim the bases. Plunge the sprouts into the boiling water and cook for 15 minutes or until fork tender. Transfer to an ice bath and cool for 10 minutes. Drain the sprouts well and pat dry. Cut each sprout in half lengthwise; separate the leaves with your fingertips and reserve.

Candy Cane Beets

Trim the stem and root ends of each beet. Place the beets in a saucepan and cover with cold salted water. Set the pan over high heat and bring to a boil; reduce heat and simmer for 40 to 50 minutes or until beets are fork tender. Remove from heat and drain. When cool enough to handle, use a clean kitchen or paper towel to rub beets to remove their skins. Slice the beets lengthwise

approximately ¼ inch (6 mm) thick. Reserve.

To Assemble

Preheat the oven to 350°F (180°C). Discard the garlic slices covering the pheasant and season both sides with salt and pepper. Heat 1 tbsp (15 mL) of the oil in each of two large skillets set over medium heat. Add 3 pheasant breasts to each pan and brown for 2 minutes per side or until golden brown. Let rest for 5 minutes. Transfer skillets to the oven (or if skillets aren't heatproof, transfer meat to a rimmed baking sheet first) and roast for 8 minutes. Before cutting, let the pheasant relax for 8 minutes in a warm area.

In a clean skillet set over medium heat, melt the butter called for in the Brussels sprouts recipe until it foams. Add the shallots and sauté for 2 minutes. Add the Brussels sprouts and cook until hot. In another clean skillet, melt the butter called for in the beet recipe, add the beet slices, and heat through. Taste and season both pans of vegetables if necessary.

Divide beets evenly to make circles on six warmed plates. Arrange some sprout leaves, cup-sides up, inside this circle. Spoon in ⅓ cup (75 mL) of warm wild rice. Cut the pheasant in half diagonally and arrange over top. Drizzle plate with sauce.

Pheasant Breast on Wild Rice, Brussels Sprouts, and Candy Cane Beets

Horse Tartar
with Pommes Pont Neuf
and Quail Egg

Beef

Beef is not my meat of choice for this tartar; but, as I mentioned earlier in this chapter, I currently make this tartar with beef since purpose-bred horsemeat is not reliably available in Canada.

While the tartar is very good with beef, this dish has a more enjoyable mouth feel when it's made with horsemeat. Horsemeat has a higher moisture content than beef and is always prepared very fresh — never aged, like beef — and you really can taste and enjoy the difference.

For 6 servings

Pommes Pont Neuf
1 lb (500 g) Yukon Gold potatoes
Vegetable oil
Salt and freshly cracked black pepper to taste

Tartar
1$\frac{1}{2}$ lbs (750 g) chilled horse or beef
    tenderloin
2 tbsp (30 mL) minced shallots
1 tbsp (15 mL) minced capers
1 tbsp (15 mL) finely diced gherkins
1 tsp (5 mL) Dijon mustard
$\frac{1}{2}$ tsp (2 mL) minced garlic
$\frac{1}{2}$ tsp (2 mL) Tabasco sauce or other hot
    pepper sauce
$\frac{1}{2}$ tsp (2 mL) Worcestershire sauce
1 tsp (5 mL) canola oil
Sea salt and freshly cracked black pepper
    to taste
6 quail egg yolks

Pommes Pont Neuf
Peel the potatoes and cut into $\frac{1}{2}$-inch (1 cm) thick rectangular logs. Place in a saucepan and cover with cold salted water. Set the pot over high heat and bring to a boil; reduce heat and simmer for 7 to 10 minutes or until the potatoes are just barely fork tender. Drain and spread the potatoes onto a paper towel–lined plate to dry.

Fill a deep-fryer with oil according to manufacturer's instructions. Heat to 375°F (190°C). Fry the dried potatoes until golden brown and crisp on the outside, from 3 to 5 minutes. Remove from the oil and blot in a paper towel–lined bowl. Season with salt and freshly cracked pepper and toss gently to coat.

Tartar
Dice the meat into small cubes ($\frac{1}{4}$ inch / $\frac{1}{2}$ cm), mince slightly afterward, and refrigerate for 10 minutes. Combine the cold meat with shallots, capers, pickles, mustard, garlic, hot pepper sauce, Worcestershire sauce, and oil. Blend gently and season with salt and pepper to taste. Serve immediately.

To Assemble
Mound equal amounts of tartar on six plates. Make an indentation in the tops using the back of a spoon; top each mound with a quail egg yolk. Arrange a stack of the Pommes Pont Neuf next to the tartar. Serve immediately.

Tips
Use a 3-inch (7.5 cm) circular metal form to arrange the tartar on the plate.

If you don't have something to use as a form, use a cookie cutter, or you can make a mould from easy-to-find materials, such as a salmon can or PVC piping:

- Cut both ends from a clean salmon can.

- Buy a 2-inch (5 cm) thick piece of 3-inch (7.5 cm) plastic PVC piping from a hardware store. Wash well before using.

Local pears, sweet and juicy in September, mature at the same time as Ontario's best blackberries.

People who know me are aware that I have an allergy to a variety of nuts and legumes. When Pangaea first opened, my kitchen policy was never to use any of the items that trigger my allergies in any of our recipes. However, as time progressed, not only did our staff become well versed in the dangers of cross-contamination, but I also gained confidence in their palates, and loosened that policy slightly.

Today, several ingredients are commonly used at Pangaea that chef de cuisine Derek Bendig or pastry chef Colen Quinn enjoy working with but that I can't taste personally. This pistachio cake is one of those recipes, and, to be honest, it smells and looks so good I'd love to try it!

And speaking of Derek, I've seen him make a full meal of these vanilla-rosemary poached pears, which isn't surprising, since I have tasted them, and I can tell you that they're quite wonderful.

For 8 servings

Poached Pears
12 cups (3 L) water
5 cups (1.25 L) granulated sugar
1 vanilla bean, halved lengthwise and scraped
1/2 cup (125 mL) freshly squeezed lemon juice
1 sprig fresh rosemary
8 small Bartlett pears

Browned Butter
1 cup (250 mL) butter
1/2 vanilla bean, scraped

Brown Butter Pistachio Cake
1 cup (250 mL) pistachio nuts
1 cup (250 mL) all-purpose flour
2 tsp (10 mL) baking powder
1/4 tsp (1 mL) salt
1/2 cup (125 mL) softened browned butter
    (see above)
1 cup (250 mL) granulated sugar
3 eggs
1 tsp (5 mL) vanilla extract
Pinch grated lemon zest
Pinch grated orange zest 1/2 cup (125 mL)
whole (homogenized) milk
1 1/2 cups (375 mL) chantilly cream
    (see page 213)

Blackberry Compote
4 cups (1 L) fresh or thawed frozen blackberries
1/4 cup (50 mL) granulated sugar
1/2 cup (125 mL) water
2 tsp (10 mL) cornstarch
1 tsp (5 mL) freshly squeezed lemon juice

Poached Pears
Combine the water, sugar, vanilla pod and scraped seeds, and lemon juice in a Dutch oven or large saucepan. Bring to a boil. Add the rosemary.

Meanwhile, peel the pears, leaving the stems attached to the fruit. Slice a small amount from the bottom of each pear so that it can stand flat. Using a grapefruit spoon, a paring knife, or a small melon baller, scoop through the bottom of each pear to remove the core. Place the pears in the hot syrup and cover with a cartouche of parchment paper (see note page 189). Bring to a boil, then reduce heat to low and simmer for 10 to 15 minutes or until the fruit is fork tender but still holds its shape. Cool to room temperature in the poaching liquid. (Can be made to this point, covered tightly, and refrigerated for up to 3 days.)

Browned Butter
Place the butter, vanilla pod, and scraped seeds in a saucepan set over medium-high heat. Cook, stirring occasionally to loosen any brown bits that collect on the bottom and sides of the saucepan, for 8 minutes or until the foam that collects on the surface of the butter is about the same colour as a walnut shell.

Remove the pan from the heat and cool to room temperature in the saucepan (if you're in a hurry, place the bottom of the saucepan in an ice bath and stir until softly set). Discard the vanilla bean. Transfer the cooled butter to a clean, dry container and refrigerate until solid, stirring occasionally to ensure butter solidifies as an even mixture. Makes 3/4 cup (175 mL).

Brown Butter Pistachio Cake
Preheat the oven to 350°F (180°C). Line the bottom of a 9-inch (23 cm) square baking pan with parchment paper. Grease the pan and paper.

Combine the nuts and flour in a food processor fitted with a metal blade. Pulse for about 1 minute or until finely ground. Add the baking powder and salt; pulse to combine.

In the bowl of a stand mixer fitted with a paddle attachment, beat the browned butter on medium-high speed until light and fluffy, about 30 seconds. Add the sugar and beat for 1 minute or until the mixture is fluffy and light in colour. Add the eggs, one at a time, blending after each on low speed. Scrape down the sides of the bowl before adding the last egg, the vanilla, and the lemon and orange zests. Beat mixture on high for 2 minutes, stopping to scrape down the bowl halfway through mixing.

Add one-third of the flour mixture and blend on low until well combined. Blend in half of the milk. Repeat until all the milk and flour mixture have been added to the batter. Scrape down the bowl and beat on medium-high for 10 seconds or until the batter is

Rosemary-Vanilla Poached Pears with Brown Butter Pistachio Cake, Chantilly Cream, and Blackberry Compote

thoroughly combined. Scrape into the prepared pan and smooth until the top is level.

Bake the cake in the preheated oven for 40 minutes or until it springs back when touched lightly on top. Cool on a rack for 20 minutes. Run a knife around the edge of the pan and turn cake out onto the rack. Cool completely, then wrap tightly in plastic wrap and chill for at least 1 hour or overnight.

Blackberry Compote
Place the blackberries in a saucepan; add the sugar. Whisk the water with the cornstarch

and lemon juice. Stir into the fruit mixture; bring to a boil. Reduce the heat and simmer for 1 to 2 minutes or until the juices are thickened and the berries glossy. Cool to room temperature. (Compote can be made to this point up to 2 days in advance and stored, tightly covered, in the refrigerator. Bring to room temperature before serving.)

To Assemble
Remove pears from poaching liquid and pat dry. Stand each pear up on the left-hand side of a large, round serving plate. Trim the browned crust from the cake (reserve for making cake crumbs or for snacking). Slice

the cake in half to make two layers. Cut each layer into 12 pieces. Place a slice of cake on each plate. Top with a dollop of chantilly cream and another piece of cake. Repeat layers and top with a final dollop of cream. Spoon some Blackberry Compote onto each plate near the cake. Place a dollop of whipped cream in front of and slightly to the right of the pear.

Tip
Use leftover brown butter for making frosting or as a spread for toast with jam.

Coronation

blue grapes arrive at the market just as berry season ends in Ontario. These wonderful, semi-seedless grapes are only available from mid-August to late September, and we make sure to buy a case of not only the first but the last harvest as well, since they have such a wonderful, tart-sweet flavour and can be used to make stunningly delicious desserts.

At every other time of year in Toronto, almost all the commercially available table grapes are imported from places such as California or Chile. Imported table grapes are considerably larger than Coronation grapes, and they have skins that cling to the flesh of the fruit. Canadian-grown blue grapes, on the other hand, are each about the size of a small marble, cluster in tight bunches on the vine, and feature "slip" skins that can easily be removed from the fruit.

Many people find the idea of a baked grape dessert a little odd. For instance, Wolf Kraus, our china supplier and a Pangaea regular, was reluctant to try this dessert. But Colen insisted, and now it's one of Wolf's favourites.

For 8 servings

Grape Sorbet
5 cups (1.25 L) Coronation grapes (approx.)
1/4 cup (60 mL) water
2 tbsp (30 mL) granulated sugar
1/4 cup (60 mL) white corn syrup

Apricot Coulis
1 1/2 cups (375 mL) water
1/2 cup (125 mL) granulated sugar
1/4 cup (60 mL) liquid honey
1/2 vanilla bean, scraped
1 1/2 tsp (7 mL) vitamin C powder (ascorbic acid powder) or Fruit-Fresh (see note page 115)
4 ripe apricots, stemmed, halved and pitted

Pastry
1/3 cup (75 mL) cold butter, cubed
1/4 cup (60 mL) granulated sugar
1 egg, beaten
1/4 tsp (1 mL) vanilla extract
1 1/4 cups (300 mL) all-purpose flour
Pinch salt

Grape Custard Filling
1/4 cup (60 mL) granulated sugar
1/2 vanilla bean, scraped
1 tbsp (15 mL) cornstarch
2/3 cup (150 mL) whipping (35%) cream
3 egg yolks
1 1/2 cups (375 mL) Coronation grapes, halved and seeded

Garnish
Confectioners' (icing) sugar
1 1/2 cups (375 mL) chantilly cream (see page 213)
Coronation grapes
Fresh spearmint sprigs

Grape Sorbet

Place the grapes and water in a saucepan; bring to a boil. Cool slightly, then pass the cooked grapes through a juicer and measure out 2 cups (500 mL) of juice. (Alternatively, purée the grapes in a high-speed blender; strain and measure out 2 cups (500 mL) of juice.)

Stir the juice with the sugar until it dissolves. Stir in the corn syrup and chill in the refrigerator until very cold.

Transfer to a chilled ice cream maker and proceed according to the manufacturer's instructions until mixture is thickened. Transfer to a tub that seals tightly and freeze until set enough to scoop. (Alternatively, transfer the cooled mixture to a shallow, non-reactive pan; place in freezer. Whisk occasionally as crystals begin to form. Continue to freeze until the mixture is set and has formed a finely grainy texture.)

Apricot Coulis

Combine the water, sugar, honey, vanilla bean and its scraped seeds, and vitamin C powder in a large saucepan. Place over high heat and bring to a boil. Add the apricots and cover the surface of the pan with a parchment paper cartouche (see note page 189).

Remove the pan from the heat and let apricots cool, submerged in the syrup, until room temperature. Blend in a high-speed blender and transfer to a clean, dry squeeze bottle. Refrigerate for up to 1 week.

Pastry

In an electric stand mixer fitted with a paddle attachment, beat the butter with the sugar on medium-high until light and fluffy; scrape down the bowl. Add the egg and vanilla and beat until well combined. Add the flour and salt and beat for 2 minutes on low speed, stopping to scrape down the bowl once, until the mixture is well combined.

Transfer the mixture to a clean surface and knead gently until a smooth ball of dough forms. Press into a disk and wrap tightly with plastic wrap. Chill for 2 hours or until firm.

On a clean work surface lightly dusted with flour, roll out the dough to 1/8-inch (3 mm) thickness. Using a 4-inch (10 cm) circular metal cutter, cut out rounds. Set eight 3 1/2-inch (9 cm) tart rings on a parchment paper–lined baking sheet. Line each ring with a round of pastry that is just slightly higher than the top of the ring. (If you like, cut circles larger and flute the top edge of the pastry.) Refrigerate for at least 30 minutes.

Preheat the oven to 350°F (180°C). Line each tart shell with parchment paper and pie weights. Bake for 20 minutes. Remove the weights, paper, and ring; let pastry cool slightly. Return to oven and bake for 15 minutes. Cool completely.

Grape Custard Filling

If necessary, preheat the oven again to 350°F (180°C). Place the sugar and vanilla

Coronation Grape Tart
with Apricot Coulis, Chantilly Cream, and Grape Sorbet

seeds in a bowl. Using your fingers, rub the seeds into the sugar until well combined. Stir in the cornstarch. Whisk in the cream and let stand for 2 minutes. Stir until sugar is dissolved; whisk egg yolks into cream mixture until combined. Can be chilled until ready to use, up to 2 days.

Meanwhile, scatter an equal number of grapes into each baked tart shell. Stir the cream mixture and pour an equal amount into each shell; fill them so the custard and grapes come to the top but aren't floating above the rim of each shell. Bake in the preheated oven for 35 minutes or until the custard is set and the grapes are bubbling.

To Assemble
On the left-hand side of eight large serving plates, place a grape tart. Squeeze a cascade of Apricot Coulis drops in descending size around the top edge of the tart. Dust the right-hand side of the plates with a little confectioners' sugar. Dip two spoons into hot water and use them to shape the chantilly cream into quenelles; place one on the right side of each plate. Garnish with a sprig of mint and a few grapes. Place a small scoop of Grape Sorbet in front of each quenelle of whipped cream.

Kataifi

is not well known, but it's time to change that situation. It is a shredded phyllo-style dough that many Middle Eastern pastry makers use to make crunchy, light coatings and shells for both sweet and savoury items. Here, pastry chef Colen Quinn uses it as a crisp, buttery foil to the cool and quivery panna cotta. By roasting the spices, Colen adds depth and a Middle Eastern flair to this classic Italian dessert, which makes it unique, surprising, and enjoyable.

Unlike many of the other desserts we serve at Pangaea, this one is ideal for home cooks who like to entertain. Every element can be made ahead so you don't have to do any last-minute preparation before plating and serving dessert.

For 8 servings

Roasted Cinnamon and Vanilla Panna Cotta

3 cinnamon sticks, each about 3 inches (7.5 cm)
1/4 tsp (1 mL) ground cinnamon
3 cups (750 mL) whipping (35%) cream
1/2 cup (125 mL) whole (homogenized) milk
1 vanilla bean, split lengthwise and scraped
1/2 cup (125 mL) granulated sugar
Pinch salt
3 tbsp (45 mL) cold water
4 tsp (20 mL) gelatin powder
1/2 cup (125 mL) chantilly cream (see page 213)

Apple and Raisin Compote

1/4 cup (60 mL) Thompson or other raisins
Boiling water
4 Gala apples, peeled, cored, and diced
1/4 cup (60 mL) lightly packed brown sugar
1 tsp (5 mL) brandy

Kataifi Disks

1 1/2 cups (375 mL) thawed pastry, about 2.5 oz (75 g)
4 tsp (20 mL) melted unsalted butter
2 tsp (10 mL) granulated sugar

Caramel Sauce

3/4 cup (175 mL) granulated sugar
Pinch salt
1/4 cup (60 mL) water
1 tsp (5 mL) freshly squeezed lemon juice
1/2 cup (125 mL) whipping (35%) cream

Roasted Cinnamon and Vanilla Panna Cotta

Break the cinnamon sticks into large chunks and place in a saucepan with the ground cinnamon; set over medium heat. Toast, shaking the pan occasionally, for 2 minutes or until very fragrant. Add the cream, milk, vanilla pod, and scraped seeds to the saucepan; whisk occasionally as you bring this mixture to a boil. Remove from the heat. Immediately add the sugar and salt. Stir until sugar is dissolved; cool until lukewarm.

Place the water in a small, heatproof bowl, or the top of a double boiler. Sprinkle the gelatin over and shake until powder is completely saturated and lump free. Let stand for 5 minutes. Set gelatin over a small saucepan filled with 1 inch (2.5 cm) of simmering water and heat, stirring, until smooth. Whisk the gelatin mixture into the cream mixture.

Pass the mixture through a fine-mesh sieve into a clean bowl; discard solids in strainer. Divide the mixture evenly among eight small, shallow bowls or ramekins with rounded bottoms. Cover and chill for 4 hours or until set. (Recipe can be prepared to this point up to 2 days in advance.)

Apple and Raisin Compote

Place raisins in a small, heatproof bowl and cover with boiling water. Let stand for 10 minutes or until plump; drain well. Squeeze out excess moisture.

Meanwhile, set a large skillet over high heat. Once the skillet is very hot, add the apples and brown sugar. Immediately start stirring; cook, stirring often, for 8 to 10 minutes or until golden. Stir in the raisins and brandy. Remove from heat; cool completely. Makes 2 cups (500 mL).

Kataifi Disks

Preheat the oven to 325°F (160°C). Line a rimmed baking sheet with parchment paper.

Working quickly, place the thawed pastry shreds in a bowl and toss to separate. Drizzle with butter and sprinkle with sugar; toss to coat evenly. Divide the pastry into 8 equal portions. Pat each portion into a 3-inch (7.5 cm) ring to form into round, thin disks; press down firmly until pastry holds its shape.

Bake in the preheated oven, rotating the pan halfway during cooking, for 12 to 15 minutes or until the disks are evenly coloured light golden; cool completely. Disks can be stored in an airtight container for up to 2 days.

Caramel Sauce

Place sugar and salt in a small, heavy-bottomed saucepan. Slowly pour water and lemon juice over sugar. Stir to combine, being careful not to splash the mixture up the sides of the pan.

Set the saucepan over high heat. Stir until the sugar completely dissolves and the mixture begins to boil around the edges. (Dissolve any sugar that begins to crystallize on the side of the pan with a pastry brush dipped in water.) Bring the mixture to a full boil and cook, without stirring but occasionally swirling the pan gently to even out the browning, for 5 to 6 minutes or until the temperature reaches 350°F (180°C) on a candy thermometer. Remove from heat and stir in the cream. Return to heat and cook, stirring, until temperature reaches 250°F (125°C). Cool to room temperature. Scrape into a clean, dry squeeze bottle. Sauce can be stored in the refrigerator for up to 5 days.

Roasted Cinnamon and Vanilla Panna Cotta with Kataifi Disks, Apple Raisin Compote, and Caramel Sauce

To Assemble

Run a thin knife around the edge of each panna cotta; slip a small rubber spatula between the bowl and the custard and invert the bowl. Use the spatula to guide the custard out of the bowl onto a serving plate. Top with a dollop of chantilly cream and then a kataifi disk. Spoon 3 small mounds of the apple compote around the panna cotta. Use the squeeze bottle to drizzle Caramel Sauce decoratively around the plate.

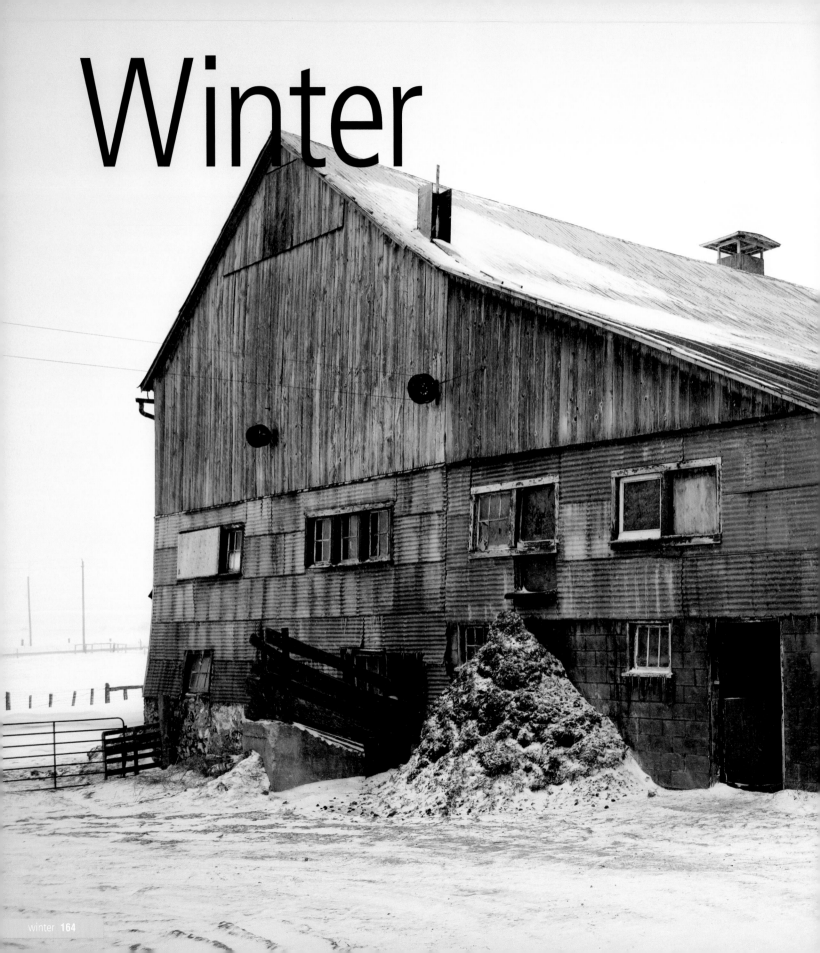

Winter

Buried Treasure

One of the things that intrigues me is how, in this day and age of technological advances and scientific breakthroughs, many of us are rediscovering that the old ways of preparing and storing foods are worth reviving. Pickling, canning, charcuterie, and cheese-making are being rediscovered by chefs and home cooks en masse.

At Cookstown Greens, organic farmer David Cohlmeyer takes things one step further. He and his team have built large, humidity-controlled root cellars so that chefs like me can have longer access to locally grown, jewel-toned root vegetables such as beets, carrots, parsnips, and turnips. In April, before the tulips have even emerged from still frozen Ontario soil, I've eaten baby candy cane beets that have wintered in David's cellar and still taste field fresh!

Whey-Fed Pork
— The Way to Go

When Pangaea opened in October 1996, pork didn't have a prominent place on our menu. At that time, finding superior-quality local pork was difficult because most Canadian swine were bred to be very lean and mild-flavoured to compete against chicken as "the other white meat." As a result, most of the pork we could find then was flavourless and dry. Those were dark days!

This lack of good local pork led me to explore the great cured-pork options the wider world had to offer. From German speck used to flavour a zesty red cabbage and venison dish on one of our first menus to imported Italian prosciutto that we draped over balsamic-drizzled mission figs, we were able to serve great cured pork. We even became the first restaurant in North America to carry the famous *jamón ibérico de bellota*, a cured, serrano-style ham made from the acorn-eating black pigs native to Spain. But despite these porcine pleasures, our hopes to use regional ingredients and offer a great pork chop went unsatisfied.

A decade later, our quality pork options were suddenly abundant. Recognition and appreci-ation of heritage pork strains and of natural methods of breeding pork had spread to Canada, and chefs were talking among themselves about pork breeds and suppliers. Today, we have a ready supply of excellent local pork that we buy whole. Some of each pig is butchered to serve fresh as chops while we preserve the rest making our own dry-cured sausages, salami, headcheese, and an

excellent prosciutto that we serve alongside the *jamón ibérico de bellota* on our popular charcuterie tasting plate.

Although we've purchased excellent artisan-raised pork from a number of farms, we have several favourite pork suppliers. Rory O'Neill raises free-range Tamworth pigs. His farm is small and only produces three or four pigs a month, so we support him when he has a pig ready at the same time that we need one. Likewise, for events where we need a special item, we buy the small, tender St-Conat Farms milk-fed piglets. They can be as old as six months, but these pigs are fed a milk diet their entire lives. They're expensive, but so tender and delicious that they're perfect for special parties.

Our most regular supplier, though, is David E.M. Martin, an old-order Mennonite who farms near St. Jacobs, Ontario. He feeds his pigs whey and raises them with absolutely no hormones or antibiotics in a lovely old, light-filled barn. Buying pork from David takes you back in time because he doesn't use a phone, computer, or any other method of electronic communication. Until recently, we had only two ways to reach him. We could call Ruth Klahsen, the owner of Monforte cheese in nearby Millbank, and ask her to drive over to David's and order us a pig. However, Ruth's business has now moved a little north to Stratford. So for a while we were left with our second option: to write David a letter and wait for him to send one back to let us know when our pig would be shipped to the abattoir and be ready for pickup.

It's certainly easier to email a wholesale butcher and order 100 pre-portioned pork chops, but for me it was always worth the extra effort of writing a letter and doing a bit of knife work to enjoy the sweet, succulent pork David E.M. Martin produces using age-old methods. Recently, a distributor heard about chefs like me who were buying pork from David and began handling his orders, so now we call them. The meat is the same as always, and the price is only a bit higher — but I actually miss writing those letters.

Never Bogged Down

Cranberries invariably show up on our winter menu at Pangaea. These berries are so versatile that we're never at a loss for ways to use them. While in this book they're used only on page 198 as a garnish for the lemon tart, we also use cranberries in savoury recipes.

As a native North American fruit, the cranberry was an important dietary staple for the indigenous people, who referred to the berries as *sassamanash*. They used cranberries in pemmican cakes, for example, prepared by combining cranberries with lean, dried strips of meat that were pounded into a paste and then mixed with animal fat and grains. This concoction sustained them during cold weather and on long journeys. Later, cranberries were used by pioneers to make dyes and poultices and became a valuable source of vitamin C for settlers, who had little access to fresh fruits and vegetables in the winter.

There are several primary cranberry-growing regions in Canada. In Ontario, cranberries grow well in the marshes near Muskoka, and the berries grow well in British Columbia, too.

It's a common misconception that cranberries grow in water. In truth, they grow on vines in beds, commonly known as bogs, that are layered with sand, peat, gravel, and clay. Preparing these growing areas is very difficult, so the only real possibility for most people to experience a scarlet harvest is to visit a commercial cranberry bog or one of the very few areas in Saskatchewan or Yukon where this fruit grows wild. The best time to make a trek to a cranberry bog is between late September and Halloween, when growers flood the fields and the fruit turns various shades of red, from rosy pink to scarlet.

Winter
recipes

Appetizers

Main Courses

Desserts

Triptych of Winter Soups
    Parsnip and Lemon with Tarragon Cream
    Cashew and Sweet Potato with Coconut Milk and Crème Fraîche
    Yellow Carrot and Crisp Ginger Chip

Root cellar

favourites like parsnips, carrots, and sweet potatoes are wintertime staples in the Pangaea kitchen.

We make a lot of soup in a day at that time of year, so although I use heirloom carrots in this yellow carrot soup, I save money by asking Cookstown Greens to send us the carrots that they grade as "seconds." All that means is that they aren't as perfectly shaped as the first-grade carrots. As a home cook, I recommend that you get to know the farmers at your local markets; if you play your cards right, I bet a basket of seconds will be made available to you at a fraction of the cost of the firsts.

For 8 servings each of three soups

Parsnip and Lemon Soup
1 tbsp (15 mL) butter
¹⁄₂ cup (125 mL) diced Spanish onion
2 cups (500 mL) peeled, diced parsnips
4 cups (1 L) chicken stock (see page 208)
1 tbsp (15 mL) grated lemon zest
³⁄₄ tsp (4 mL) salt or to taste

Tarragon Cream
¹⁄₂ cup (125 mL) whipping (35%) cream
1 tsp (5 mL) chopped fresh tarragon leaves

Cashew and Sweet Potato Soup with Coconut Milk and Crème Fraîche
1 lb (500 g) sweet potatoes, about 1 large
1 tbsp (15 mL) butter
¹⁄₂ cup (125 mL) diced Spanish onion
3 cups (750 mL) chicken stock (see page 208)
¹⁄₂ cup (125 mL) unsalted roasted cashews
2 tsp (10 mL) grated lime zest
¹⁄₂ cup (125 mL) coconut milk
1 tsp (5 mL) salt or to taste

Garnish
¹⁄₄ cup (60 mL) crème fraîche (see page 90)
    or sour cream
1 tsp (5 mL) chervil or tiny cilantro leaves

Parsnip and Lemon Soup
In a large saucepan set over medium heat, melt the butter until it foams, then add the onions and sauté for about 3 minutes until tender. Add the parsnip and stock and bring to a boil; stir in the lemon zest. Reduce the heat and simmer for 15 minutes. Remove from heat and cool slightly.

In a high-speed blender, purée the soup and season with salt. Pass the mixture through a medium strainer; taste and adjust seasoning if necessary.

Tarragon Cream
In a chilled stainless-steel bowl, whip the cream until stiff. Fold in the chopped tarragon and refrigerate for up to 2 hours.

Cashew and Sweet Potato Soup with Coconut Milk and Crème Fraîche
Preheat oven to 350°F (180°C). Bake the sweet potato until soft, about 80 to 90 minutes. Remove from the oven and cool until safe to handle. Peel and discard the skin; chop potato.

In a large saucepan set over medium heat, heat the butter until it foams; add the onions and sauté for about 3 minutes or until tender. Add the reserved sweet potato, stock, cashews, and lime zest. Bring to a boil, then reduce heat and simmer for 30 minutes. Remove from the heat, cool slightly, then stir in the coconut milk.

In a high-speed blender, purée the soup and season with salt. Pass the mixture through a medium strainer; taste and adjust seasoning if necessary.

To Serve
Warm three small bowls per person. Spoon out even portions of the three soups and garnish with appropriate toppings.

Tips
If a soup thickens as it sits, adjust the texture by adding a little boiling water.

For vegetarian versions, substitute vegetable broth or water for the chicken stock.

Yellow Carrot Soup

1 tbsp (15 mL) butter
¼ cup (60 mL) finely diced white onion
2½ cups (625 mL) peeled, diced yellow
    carrots
¼ cup (60 mL) white wine, divided
1 tbsp (15 mL) liquid honey
2 tsp (10 mL) minced fresh ginger
¾ tsp (4 mL) ground cardamom
½ tsp (2 mL) ground cumin
1 tsp (5 mL) red wine vinegar
4 cups (1 L) chicken stock (see page 208)
¾ tsp (4 mL) salt or to taste

Garnish
Crisp Candied Ginger (see page 212)

Yellow Carrot Soup

Melt the butter over medium heat. Add the
onions and cook for 2 minutes or until
translucent. Add the carrots and cook for
3 minutes longer. Add half the wine and cook
for 2 minutes. Stir in the honey, minced
ginger, cardamom, and cumin. Add the rest
of the white wine along with the vinegar;
boil until the liquid is reduced slightly. Add
the chicken stock and salt; bring to a boil,
then reduce the heat so that the mixture
simmers rapidly but doesn't splatter and boil
uncontrollably. Cook, stirring occasionally,
for 20 to 25 minutes or until the carrots are
very tender.

Remove from heat and cool slightly. Purée
in a high-speed blender until smooth. Taste
and adjust seasoning if necessary. Pass
the purée through a fine-mesh strainer and
reheat until very hot.

Crab Cake
with Fennel Slaw
and Tomato and Ginger Jam

For 10 servings

Crab Cakes
1 tbsp (15 mL) canola oil
1 cup (250 mL) carrots, peeled and diced
   (measure after prep)
1 cup (250 mL) celery, diced
1 cup (250 mL) onion, diced
2 cups (500 mL) white wine
1 bay leaf
3 tbsp (45 mL) whole black peppercorns
32 cups (8 L) water
3/4 cup (175 mL) salt
2 Dungeness crabs, each 2½ lbs (1.5 kg)
½ cup green onion, sliced thin
Zest of 6 small limes, about 2 tbsp (30 mL)
½ cup (125 mL) mayonnaise
2½ cups (625 mL) panko bread crumbs, divided
Salt and freshly ground black pepper
Canola oil
Fennel fronds

Fennel Slaw
1 bulb fennel
1 tbsp (15 mL) capers
1 tsp (5 mL) chives
1 tbsp (15 mL) canola oil
1 tsp (5 mL) freshly squeezed lemon juice
Salt and freshly ground black pepper to taste

Horseradish-Shallot Vinaigrette
2 tbsp (30 mL) red wine vinegar
1 tbsp (15 mL) grated fresh or prepared
   horseradish
2 tsp (10 mL) minced shallots
¼ tsp (1 mL) salt or to taste
¼ tsp (1 mL) freshly ground black pepper
   or to taste
½ tsp (2 mL) Dijon mustard
¼ cup (60 mL) canola oil

Tomato and Ginger Jam
2 tsp (10 mL) butter
1 tsp (5 mL) minced shallot
1 tsp (5 mL) minced garlic
5 plum (Roma) tomatoes, peeled, seeded
   and finely diced, about 2 cups (500 mL)
1 tbsp (15 mL) granulated sugar
2 tsp (10 mL) minced fresh ginger
1 tsp (5 mL) freshly squeezed lemon juice
2 tsp (18 mL) freshly squeezed lime juice
2 tsp (10 mL) finely chopped fresh tarragon leaves
Salt and freshly ground white pepper to taste

Dungeness

crab is one of the crown jewels of the Pacific Ocean; it has succulent, pink flesh that's truly delicious. Beyond this great main ingredient, the appeal of this recipe over other crab cakes I've tried lies in the way the flavours play off one another. Sweet, tangy, fresh, and savoury come together in delicious harmony.

I always use trap-caught Dungeness crab, since this harvesting method allows the fishers to release any bycatch and harvest only 6¼ inch (16 cm) or larger male crabs.

After making this recipe hundreds of times, I know that an average Dungeness crab yields enough meat to make 5 crab cakes, so I'm calling for 2 crabs. And instead of publishing a recipe that leaves you with leftover ingredients, this particular recipe makes 10 portions. If you don't have enough friends to necessitate making 10 crab cakes, just save some of the raw mixture to cook the next day. These crab cakes are so good that you'll likely want more anyhow.

When cooking crab or lobster, you'll get the best results if the cooking liquid tastes about as salty as the ocean, so don't be alarmed by the amount of salt called for in this recipe. That's really how much you need.

Crab Cakes

Heat the oil in a large stockpot set over medium-high heat. When the oil is hot, add the carrots, celery, and onion. When the vegetables begin to sizzle, stir well and cover pot; cook for 2 minutes. Deglaze the pan with white wine; add the bay leaf and peppercorns and allow the liquid to reduce by half. Add the water and bring to a boil.

Add the salt to the boiling water and plunge the crabs into the mixture; return to a boil and cook for 10 minutes. Plunge the crab into an ice bath consisting of equal parts ice and water. After 10 minutes, remove the crabs from the ice bath. Crack the shells and remove the meat (use a wooden skewer to help coax the meat out of the nooks and crannies). Chill the crabmeat completely in the refrigerator. Once thoroughly chilled, pick over the meat to check for any wayward bits of shell. Drain well.

Add the green onions, lime zest, and mayonnaise to the crabmeat; gently fold together. Add ½ cup (125 mL) of the panko bread crumbs and blend evenly. Season with salt and pepper to taste. Form the crab mixture into 10 equal balls. Flatten each ball into a puck shape and coat all over with the remaining bread crumbs. Place the cakes on a parchment paper–lined tray; cover and chill.

Fennel Slaw

Trim and discard the base of the fennel bulb. Trim the fronds and reserve some to garnish the plates. Using a meat slicer or a mandoline, slice the fennel crosswise into long, thin pieces. Chop the capers, slice the chives into short lengths, and toss with the fennel. Drizzle with oil and lemon juice and toss well. Do not season until just before serving.

Horseradish-Shallot Vinaigrette

In a small bowl, whisk together the vinegar, horseradish, and shallots. Season with salt and pepper. Add the mustard and whisk in the oil. Refrigerate for 1 hour and then strain. Taste and adjust seasoning if necessary. Refrigerate until ready for use.

Tomato and Ginger Jam

In a skillet set over medium heat, melt the butter until it foams. Add the shallot and garlic and sauté for 1 to 2 minutes or until tender. Add the tomatoes, sugar, ginger, and lemon juice and cook for about 15 minutes or until the pan starts to become dry.

Remove from heat and add lime juice and tarragon and combine well. Season with salt and pepper to taste and cool. Place the tomato and ginger jam into a storage container, cover tightly, and refrigerate until needed.

To Assemble

Heat a skillet over medium-high heat. Brush with enough vegetable oil to coat well. Working in batches and adding more oil as necessary, fry the crab cakes until golden brown, about 3 to 4 minutes on each side.

In a small bowl, combine the fennel with Horseradish-Shallot Vinaigrette; season to taste and toss well. Place a small mound in the centre of each of ten serving plates; place a crab cake on top. Using two teaspoons, form quenelles with the Tomato Ginger Jam and drop one in the centre of each crab cake. Garnish with fennel fronds and serve.

Grilled Calamari
with Anchovies, Olives,
Roasted Garlic, Lemon, Tomato,
Onion, and Capers in Brown Butter

Squid is at its very best — toothsome, tender, and delicious — in

this succulent dish. In fact, I still crave it myself, even though I've been making it on a regular basis for almost 20 years. Each flavour is present and accounted for without overpowering another. The various elements come together like a harmony of individual voices in a choir. In other words, it's really good!

I first developed this recipe when I worked at Pronto Ristorante in Toronto. Often, I go to another restaurant and see a variation of my recipe on the menu. Instead of being miffed that my idea has been copied, I'm gratified. After all, once you taste this yummy concoction, how can you be blamed for wanting to share it with others?

One aspect of this dish that I would like to see everyone who makes it duplicate is to buy squid that is caught using low-bycatch jigs or trawls operated by harvesters who know to leave enough squid in a fishing area so that the local ocean species who use them as food will have a dinner, too.

For 4 servings

Grilled Calamari
8 whole squid, about 1³/₄ lbs (800 g) in total
1 tbsp (15 mL) minced garlic
1 tbsp (15 mL) minced jalapeño pepper
1 tbsp (15 mL) canola oil
¹/₂ tsp (2 mL) freshly grated nutmeg
2 lemons, halved

Browned Butter
¹/₂ cup (125 mL) butter

Vegetables
¹/₂ cup (125 mL) halved cherry tomatoes
    or peeled, seeded, diced plum (Roma)
    tomatoes
1 tbsp (15 mL) finely chopped lemon zest
2 tbsp (30 mL) freshly squeezed lemon juice
4 anchovy fillets, minced, or 2 tbsp (30 mL)
    anchovy paste
¹/₄ cup (60 mL) small capers
¹/₂ cup (125 mL) Gaeta, Kalamata, or other
    firm black olives
12 cloves roasted garlic (see page 212)
¹/₄ cup (60 mL) finely diced red onion

Calamari
Pull the skin off the body (mantle) of each squid. Rinse with water. Cut the head off just below the eyes and discard eyes. With two fingers, press the round sac that contains the beak to remove. Discard beak and reserve tentacles. Remove the clear pen-like shell from the body cavity of each squid and discard. Using a sharp knife, slice a ¹/₄-inch (6 mm) wide fringe along the side of each body. Reserve along with the tentacles.

Browned Butter
In a dry saucepan set over high heat, melt the butter; simmer, skimming off and discarding the foam (tilt the pan to make it easier to skim off the last few solids that rise to the top). Cook butter for 3 to 4 minutes or until the butter turns a light, nutty brown colour; remove from heat and cool slightly. Pour slowly into a bowl, making sure the sediment remains in the bottom of the pan. Discard the sediment. Reserve clarified brown butter.

Grilled Calamari
Toss sliced bodies and tentacles with garlic, jalapeño, canola oil, and nutmeg to coat lightly. Heat the grill until very hot; wipe the grate off with an oil-soaked rag. Grill calamari over high heat for 2 minutes per side or until slightly charred.

Vegetables
Meanwhile, in a large skillet, combine the reserved brown butter, tomatoes, lemon zest, lemon juice, anchovies, capers, olives, roasted garlic, and onions. Cook over medium-high heat for 1 minute or until very hot.

To Assemble
Divide the calamari among four serving plates and drizzle evenly with brown butter mixture. Garnish each serving with half a lemon.

Wild Capers
Used often in the sun-drenched cuisines of southern Italy and France, capers are a wonderful, versatile ingredient. I often use this imported Mediterranean ingredient in my signature grilled calamari, but through Jonathan Forbes of Forbes Wild Foods, I discovered several Canadian versions of capers that we use in many of our other recipes. See page 38 for more information about the capers you can make from the buds of Ontario meadow flowers.

Saint-Simon Oysters
on the Half Shell with Wine
and Shallot Mignonette

East Coast

oysters are the ones I love best. They're so plump, juicy, and fresh-tasting. Not surprisingly, everyone from the West Coast who works in our kitchen begs to differ!

Saint-Simon oysters are cultured in the south bay of Saint-Simon Inlet, in northeastern New Brunswick. This isolated area is surrounded by salty marshlands that act as a natural filter, so this water is pollution free. We buy from a company established in 1973 by the Mallet family. Their oysters are cultured from "seeds" captured in Caraquet Bay and transferred to the Shippagan area, where they are cultured.

The term "oyster seed" refers to baby oysters that are transplanted in another location for the purposes of commercial grow-out or restoration. Although some companies use seed produced in a hatchery, Saint-Simon oyster seed is harvested from the wild.

The farming process is fascinating. The seed oysters are raised in crates that float lower and rise with the tide. This process prevents the oysters from becoming gritty like sand-bed-raised oysters and ensures that they never come into contact with any refuse that may rest on the ocean floor.

When selecting oysters, choose specimens that are heavy for their size and have tightly closed and undamaged shells. At home, store them in the coldest part of the fridge with the cup, or rounded side, down to retain their natural juices. Drape the container in a wet towel topped with a little ice. And remember, don't submerge the oysters in water or cover them with plastic wrap!

For 4 servings

Wine and Shallot Mignonette
¼ cup (60 mL) dry white wine
2 tbsp (30 mL) red wine vinegar
1 tbsp (15 mL) minced shallots
¼ tsp (1 mL) freshly cracked black pepper
½ tsp (2 mL) chopped fresh tarragon leaves

Oysters
4 cups (1 L) crushed ice or freezer-chilled, clean river pebbles
16 Saint-Simon or other cold-water Canadian oysters
Lemon wedges
Freshly grated horseradish

Wine and Shallot Mignonette
Combine the wine, vinegar, and shallots. Add black pepper. Refrigerate until chilled through or for up to 2 days. Stir in tarragon just before serving.

To Assemble
Spread the ice or frozen pebbles on a large, shallow platter. Shuck the oysters using an oyster-shucking knife (see box below). Arrange opened oysters in their shells on the pebbles. Serve the mignonette in a small pitcher or ramekin, along with the lemon wedges and a small ramekin of horseradish on the side.

Tip
I buy polished and unpolished river stones at the aquarium supply store. We wash them well and dry them and store them in the freezer to use as a drip-free base that keeps our oysters super chilled when they're served.

How to Shuck an Oyster
To ensure safety, on a flat surface, use a clean dishtowel to hold each oyster with the cup-side down. Work the tip of the oyster knife sideways into the hinge (the little groove at the base of each oyster) until it is firmly planted. Turn the shucking blade up toward the body of the oyster to separate the shells slightly, then slide the blade along the length of each shell to cut the top of the small, round muscle that connects the oyster to its shell. Discard the top shells and then slide the oyster knife underneath the bottom muscle to free the oyster from the shell.

Roasted Chèvre and Beet Salad
with Candied Ginger

Crunch

is added to this salad without using croutons or nuts. Instead, we make a tissue-paper-thin candied ginger garnish that adds flavour and crunch without making the salad too heavy. I use Woolwich Dairy's chèvre for this recipe. It has a compact, smooth texture and a lower fat content than many similar goat cheeses, and that lower fat content is a big plus when roasting because the heat doesn't cause the cheese to become molten and flow away.

For 6 servings

Beet Salad

4 large red or yellow beets, about 10 oz
    (300 g) each
3 tbsp (45 mL) red wine vinegar
2 tsp (10 mL) salt
Sea salt and freshly ground black pepper
2 cups (500 mL) mixed salad greens
12 oz (340 g) chèvre, preferably local
1 tbsp (15 mL) Red Wine Vinaigrette
    (see recipe below)
1/2 cup (125 mL) lightly packed radish sprouts
Crisp Candied Ginger (see page 212)

Red Wine Vinaigrette

2 tbsp (30 mL) red wine vinegar
1/2 tsp (2 mL) Dijon mustard
1/4 tsp (1 mL) sea salt
1/4 tsp (1 mL) freshly ground black pepper
1/2 cup (125 mL) extra virgin olive oil

Beet Salad

Place the beets in a pot and cover with cold water. Add the vinegar and salt. Bring to a boil; reduce heat to a simmer. Cover and cook beets for 60 minutes or until fork tender. Remove from cooking liquid and cool until you can handle them easily. Use a clean kitchen cloth or paper towel to rub away the skins.

Slice the peeled beets into thin rounds, each about 1/16 inch (1 mm) thick, using a mandoline or a meat slicer set on 1. Using a 7-inch (18 cm) plate, trace a circle onto a sheet of parchment paper. (This will be your template for the beet mats.) Place a second piece of parchment paper over the template and carefully arrange the beet rounds in concentric circles, beginning from the centre and moving outward, overlapping the beets and covering the edge of the template so no outline is visible. Place the plate over the beets and, using a very sharp paring knife, cut around the plate so you have a perfect circle of beets underneath. Repeat with layers of parchment paper and beets until you have six stacked portions. (Portions can be stacked and tightly wrapped in plastic and refrigerated for up to 24 hours.)

Dip a sharp knife in boiling water and wipe dry. Slice goat cheese into 6 equal-sized disks. Using your hands, shape each portion into a round puck. Cover and refrigerate.

Red Wine Vinaigrette

Whisk the vinegar with the mustard, salt, and pepper until well combined. Whisk in the oil until just combined. Store in the refrigerator for up to 2 days.

To Assemble

Preheat the broiler to high.

Season the beet mats lightly. Turn the beet mats, vegetable-side down, over six large dinner plates; carefully peel away the parchment. Clean any beet juice from the plate rims if necessary.

Lightly oil a small metal baking sheet; arrange the chèvre on the tray. Broil for 5 minutes or until the cheese is golden brown on top.

Meanwhile, toss the greens with enough of the vinaigrette to dress lightly. Place a small mound of salad greens in the middle of each beet mat. Place each piece of cheese in the centre of the salad greens. Drizzle additional vinaigrette over the beets and garnish with candied ginger; serve while the cheese is still warm.

Tip

For a more relaxed presentation (like the one pictured on page 186), thinly slice the beets and pat dry, then drape them over one another, folding slightly to create a ruffled edge.

Oxtail

may be a lowly peasant food, but by pairing it with a gourmet ingredient like white truffles, I find this pasta recipe to be very democratic. As observers of international politics can tell you, establishing a democracy takes time. So be prepared to plan ahead when you make this recipe. You'll need at least two days to marinate the meat, simmer, and chill it, and then another day to form the ravioli.

I'd like to say that I'm immune to fads, but the truth is, I'm as curious and charmed by novelty as the next person. In fact, I flirted with foam as a food garnish myself for a while. Today, the only dish we still garnish with foam is this one. In this case, it really works, and it gives us something to do with the cooking liquid we have left over when we make celeriac purée (see page 108). It's quite easy to make. Just fit a hand-held immersion blender with a frothing blade and beat the celeriac cooking liquid until airy and bubbly. Spoon a dollop in the middle of the ravioli dish before shaving the white truffles over it.

For 6 servings

Marinade
2 cups (500 mL) red wine
1/3 cup (75 mL) diced carrot
1/3 cup (75 mL) diced celery
1/3 cup (75 mL) diced onion
1 tbsp (15 mL) chopped fresh thyme leaves
2 tsp (10 mL) minced garlic
2 tsp (10 mL) cracked black peppercorns
2 bay leaves

Oxtail
2 lbs (1 kg) oxtail pieces (typically cut in 3-inch (7.5 cm) lengths)
2 tbsp (30 mL) canola oil (approx.)
1/4 cup (60 mL) all-purpose flour
1/2 cup (125 mL) red wine
2 cups (500 mL) veal stock (see page 210) (approx.)
1 tbsp (15 mL) butter
4 tsp (20 mL) minced shallot
1 1/2 tsp (7 mL) minced garlic
2 tbsp (30 mL) thinly sliced green onion
1/2 tsp (2 mL) salt or to taste
1/4 tsp (1 mL) freshly ground black pepper or to taste

Pasta Dough
2 1/2 cups (625 mL) all-purpose flour
1 tsp (5 mL) salt
1/4 cup (60 mL) water
4 egg yolks
1/4 cup (60 mL) olive oil

Pasta
Cornmeal
3 whole eggs, beaten

Garnish (optional)
White truffle

Marinade
In a large saucepan, combine the red wine, carrots, celery, onion, thyme, garlic, cracked pepper, and bay leaves. Bring to a boil; reduce the heat and simmer for 5 minutes. Remove from heat; cool to room temperature. Transfer to a large bowl. Cover and chill in the refrigerator.

Oxtail
Rinse the oxtail pieces under cold running water and pat dry. Place in the marinade; cover tightly and marinate in the refrigerator for 1 day.

The next day, remove the oxtail from the marinade and pat dry. Reserve. Strain the marinade, separating the liquid from the vegetables. Reserve both separately. Place the marinade in a saucepan and bring to gentle simmer. Skim off any foam that develops on top and discard. Continue simmering and

skimming for at least 15 minutes. Strain through a fine-mesh sieve. Reserve liquid.

Preheat the oven to 350°F (180°C). Place a large, wide saucepan over medium-high heat; add 1 tbsp (15 mL) canola oil. Dust the oxtail pieces evenly with the flour. Working in batches, add the oxtail to the pan and sear until evenly browned, about 6 to 7 minutes. Transfer browned pieces of meat to a platter and add additional oil to the pan between batches if necessary. Deglaze the pan with the red wine, stirring with a wooden spoon to scrape up the cooked-on bits. Simmer to reduce the wine by about half.

Stir in the reserved marinade mixture and simmer to reduce by half. Add browned oxtail, the vegetables from the marinade, and the veal stock; bring to a boil. Fit a cartouche (see note page 189) into the pan and transfer the mixture to the oven for 2 1/2 to 3 hours or until the meat is so tender that it is falling off the bones. Remove from oven and cool to room temperature.

In a hot skillet set over medium heat, add the butter. Once the butter foams, add the shallots, garlic, and green onions and cook for 8 minutes or until very soft.

Meanwhile, shake each piece of oxtail gently to remove and separate the meat from the bones and gristle. Place the meat into a stand mixer fitted with a paddle attachment. Mix on medium speed until the meat is finely shredded and resembles pulled pork. Blend in the sautéed shallot mixture. Transfer to a tightly covered container and refrigerate until fully chilled or for up to 24 hours.

Strain the oxtail braising liquid through a fine-mesh sieve five times and then strain through damp cheesecloth into a saucepan; place over medium-high heat. Just before it comes to a boil, reduce heat and simmer for about 1 hour to reduce the liquid by half. Taste and adjust the seasoning with salt and pepper if necessary.

Pasta Dough
Combine flour with salt and mix well. Make a well in flour mixture and pour in water, egg yolks, and olive oil. Stir to make a ragged

Oxtail Ravioli with White Truffle

dough. Knead on a floured surface for 3 to 5 minutes or until smooth. Wrap tightly in plastic wrap and let rest for 2 hours at room temperature.

Clamp and secure a pasta roller to a stand mixer (or use a hand cranked pasta machine). Dust a large, clean work surface with flour. Position the pasta maker so that it is at one end of the flour-dusted counter. Divide the dough into 4 pieces, 5 to 6 oz (150 to 175 g) each, about the size of a small orange. Cover the pasta dough with a damp cloth.

Flatten each portion of dough into a long, thin rectangle about 1¹/₂-inches (4 cm) wide at the narrow ends. Adjust the pasta machine to its widest setting and roll the pasta dough through onto the dusted counter. Dial the setting down a notch and roll dough through onto the counter again. Continue until you get to setting 7 or until the dough is translucent and 3¹/₂ inches (9 cm) wide. Dust lightly on both sides with flour and fold lightly. Cover with a damp cloth. Repeat with each portion of dough.

Pasta

Line a large rimmed baking sheet with parchment paper and sprinkle lightly with cornmeal or additional flour. Top with another piece of parchment paper.

Form the reserved oxtail meat into tightly rolled balls, using about 2 tsp (10 mL) for each.

Unfold one sheet of the pasta over a lightly floured work surface (add additional flour whenever necessary to prevent sticking). Brush lightly all over with the beaten egg. Starting in the centre, place 9 balls of oxtail meat about 1¹/₂ inches (4 cm) apart down one side of the pasta. Fold the other end of the pasta over the meat, leaving a ¹/₂-inch (1 cm) space before the first ball of meat. Gently stretch the top layer of pasta, if necessary, so that the top and bottom layers are of equal width. Use your fingers to gently mould the top layer of pasta around each ball of meat. Using a 2¹/₂-inch (6 cm) cookie cutter, cut around each piece of meat. Pick up each ravioli and gently but firmly press the pasta edges together, being careful to remove any air bubbles and to centre the meat in the pasta as much as possible. Place each ravioli between the sheets of parchment paper on the prepared baking

sheet. Let ravioli stand for at least 30 minutes or until the egg has dried enough to set.

To Assemble

Fill a Dutch oven or stockpot with salted water and bring to a boil. Cook up to 12 ravioli at a time for 6 to 8 minutes or until pasta is cooked to al dente. Transfer cooked ravioli to a lightly buttered bowl using a slotted spoon and cover loosely.

Meanwhile, skim off and discard any fat that has collected on top of the oxtail sauce and heat in a skillet set over medium heat. Keep warm.

When all the ravioli are cooked, toss to coat the ravioli in the sauce. Divide the ravioli among six heated bowls. Garnish with shaved white truffles (if using). Serve at once.

Note

A cartouche, from the Italian word *carta*, meaning "paper," is an ungreased circle of parchment or wax paper cut to fit the inside circumference of a pot to prevent food from floating above the surface of the liquid as the food cooks.

Duck Confit
with Apple-Braised Cabbage

The Brome Lake Ducks farm in

Knowlton, Quebec, flourishes on long-standing tradition. Established in 1912 on the western shore of the lake, it's Canada's oldest duck-breeding farm.

One of the many reasons Pangaea is a Brome Lake Ducks customer is that their birds are raised under humane conditions, where they fatten naturally on a daily menu consisting of a mash of cereals and soy enriched with vitamins and minerals to produce succulent meat.

For 6 servings

Duck Confit
6 duck legs, preferably from Brome Lake
    Ducks, about 4 lbs (2 kg) in total
1/4 cup (60 mL) kosher salt
1 1/2 tsp (7 mL) chopped fresh thyme leaves
1 1/2 tsp (7 mL) juniper berries, crushed
1 1/2 tsp (7 mL) cracked black peppercorns
24 cloves garlic, peeled
1 bay leaf, crumbled
8 cups (2 L) rendered duck fat (see note this page)

Apple-Braised Cabbage
1 small white cabbage, about 2 lbs (1 kg)
1 tbsp (15 mL) canola oil
1/2 cup (125 mL) diced smoked bacon,
    about 3 oz (90 g)
1 cup (250 mL) diced onion
1 tsp (5 mL) minced garlic
3/4 cup (175 mL) Riesling or other off-dry
    white wine
1/2 cup (125 mL) apple juice
1 tart local apple, diced
3 juniper berries, lightly crushed
1 bay leaf
1 piece cinnamon stick, about 1 inch (2.5 cm)
1/4 cup (60 mL) white wine vinegar (approx.)
1/4 cup (60 mL) granulated sugar (approx.)
1 tsp (5 mL) salt or to taste
1/8 tsp (1 mL) freshly ground black pepper or
    to taste

Duck Confit
Rinse the duck legs under cold water and pat dry with paper towels. Mix the salt, thyme, crushed juniper berries, and cracked pepper together; rub this mixture evenly into the skin, covering each duck leg. Arrange the duck in a single layer in a roasting pan or ovenproof casserole dish. Sprinkle garlic cloves and bay leaf over the meat. Cover tightly with plastic wrap and set aside to cure at room temperature for 45 minutes. Transfer to the refrigerator and reserve overnight or for as long as 24 hours.

Preheat the oven to 275°F (140°C). Remove duck and garlic from the pan; rinse the duck and garlic cloves well and pat dry.

Over medium-low heat, heat the duck fat in a large, deep skillet until melted. Add the duck and garlic. Increase the heat to medium-high and bring to a simmer. Cover pan tightly with foil or a snug lid and transfer to the preheated oven. Braise for 2 to 2 1/2 hours or until meat is fork tender. Remove from the oven and cool until skillet can be safely handled. Remove and discard the garlic. Transfer the duck to a clean, dry container. Strain the fat through a cheesecloth-lined sieve and reserve.

Raise the oven temperature to 450°F (230°C) and place a rack in the middle of the oven. Spread the duck legs evenly on a baking tray or broiling pan. Place the duck on the middle rack and roast until the skin is crisp and golden brown, about 20 to 25 minutes.

Apple-Braised Cabbage
Cut the cabbage into quarters; remove the core and shred, using a chef's knife or food processor, until you have 10 cups (2.5 L).

Heat the oil in a large, deep skillet or Dutch oven set over medium-high heat. Add the bacon and onion and sauté for 2 to 3 minutes or until bacon begins to brown. Add the garlic. Stir in the cabbage, wine, apple juice, apple, lightly crushed juniper berries, bay leaf, and cinnamon stick. Stir in the vinegar and sugar. Bring to a boil, then lower the heat to medium-low. Cover the pot and braise for about 60 minutes or until the cabbage is tender.

Taste the cabbage and add as much salt and pepper as necessary; likewise, add more vinegar or sugar as needed to strike a sweet-and-sour balance. (The cabbage can be prepared up to several hours in advance and rewarmed just before serving.)

To Assemble
Place a mound of cabbage in the centre of a serving plate and top with a leg of crisp duck confit.

Tip
If making the duck ahead, pour the strained fat back over the duck legs so they're covered by at least 2 inches (5 cm). Cool the meat completely in the fat. (The duck confit will keep like this in the refrigerator for up to 6 months.)

Note
Rendered duck fat can be purchased at some specialty butchers and markets or it can be made at home.

Slow-Braised Lamb Shank
with Braised Fennel
and Blue Cheese Barley

For 6 servings

Citrus Coriander Gremolata
¹/₂ cup (125 mL) chopped fresh coriander leaves
¹/₂ cup (125 mL) chopped fresh parsley leaves
2 tbsp (30 mL) finely grated lime zest,
    about 2 limes
2 tbsp (30 mL) finely grated lemon zest
2 tbsp (30 mL) finely grated orange zest
1 tsp (5 mL) ground coriander
1 tbsp (15 mL) chopped garlic

Lamb Shanks
6 lamb shanks, about 1 lb (500 g) each
2 tbsp (30 mL) canola oil (approx.)
1 cup (250 mL) chopped carrots
1 cup (250 mL) chopped onion
1 cup (250 mL) chopped celery
6 cloves garlic, peeled
2 tbsp (30 mL) tomato paste
1 cup (250 mL) red wine
1 tsp (5 mL) salt or to taste
2 tsp (10 mL) whole black peppercorns
2 cups (1.5 L) lamb, veal, or chicken stock
    (see pages 208–10), (approx.)

Fennel
3 small bulbs fennel, trimmed and peeled
    where necessary
¹/₄ cup (60 mL) Pernod or other anise-
    flavoured liqueur
2 tbsp (30 mL) canola oil
2 tsp (10 mL) granulated sugar
1 tbsp (15 mL) minced fresh ginger
¹/₂ tsp (2 mL) freshly squeezed lemon juice
¹/₂ tsp (2 mL) salt
¹/₄ tsp (1 mL) freshly ground white pepper

Blue Cheese Barley
1 cup (250 mL) pearl barley
1 tbsp (15 mL) butter
¹/₃ cup (75 mL) finely chopped onion
4 cloves garlic, minced
2 sprigs fresh rosemary
3 cups (750 mL) chicken stock (see page 208)
¹/₂ cup (125 mL) grated Parmesan cheese
1 cup (250 mL) crumbled Canadian blue cheese
¹/₃ cup (75 mL) chopped fresh parsley leaves
Salt and freshly cracked black pepper

Barley

Barley is grown in abundance in Canada. In fact, according to the University of Regina, an organization I have no cause to doubt, barley is the second most widely grown cereal in Canada after wheat. While most Canadians eat foods that contain wheat on a daily basis, not too many of us are eating homemade or manufactured foods that contain barley. That's a shame, since barley is nutritious, incredibly inexpensive, and really delicious. The only thing that consoles me is that breweries that make fantastic micro-brewed Canadian beer use so much of our national barley crop!

I like to use Ontario lamb to make this recipe since one shank is a hearty portion for one person. If only New Zealand lamb is available to you, use 12 shanks and serve each person two.

Citrus Coriander Gremolata

In a small metal bowl, combine all the ingredients together and mix thoroughly. Reserve.

Lamb Shanks

Rinse the shanks under cold running water; drain and pat dry with paper towels. Preheat the oven to 300°F (150°C).

Set a 5-quart (5 L) Dutch oven, or another saucepan large enough to hold all the lamb shanks, over high heat; add half the oil. Brown shanks, turning frequently, until well browned on all sides, about 5 minutes; work in batches and add oil if necessary. Remove shanks from the pot and transfer to a platter. Tent with foil.

Toss the carrots, onions, celery, and garlic into the hot pan. Sauté for 2 minutes. Reduce the heat to medium and stir in the tomato paste. Using a flat, stiff, heatproof spatula, or wooden spoon, scrape the bottom of the pot as you cook for 2 minutes. At the first sign of scorching, deglaze the pan with a splash of the red wine. Continue to cook until the tomato paste darkens and is almost brown. Pour in the remaining wine; mix well. Simmer for 10 minutes or until this liquid is reduced by half.

Return the shanks to the cooking pot, stacking them like a cord of wood if necessary. Add the salt and peppercorns and pour in enough stock to cover (add extra if necessary). Bring to a boil over high heat; cover and transfer to the preheated oven. Braise for 1½ hours. Skim the top of the braising liquid and remove accumulated oil. Stir in all but 2 tbsp (30 mL) of the reserved gremolata. (The braised lamb can be made and heated again when required. In fact, the flavours develop wonderfully overnight. Cool to room temperature; transfer to a storage container with a tight lid and refrigerate until needed.)

Fennel

Preheat the oven to 400°F (200°C). Line a large rimmed baking sheet with parchment paper. Stand the fennel upright on its base and cut down through the root into ½-inch (1 cm) thick slices, so that the slices stay attached at their base.

Combine the Pernod, oil, sugar, ginger, lemon juice, salt, and pepper; pour over the fennel. Roast, turning once, for 30 to 35 minutes or until fork tender and golden brown.

Blue Cheese Barley

Place the barley in a strainer and rinse under cold running water; drain well. In a saucepan set over high heat, melt the butter until it foams; add the onion and sauté for 1 minute. Add the barley, garlic, rosemary, and stock and bring to a boil. Reduce the heat and simmer, covered, for 25 minutes, stirring occasionally. Remove lid; remove and discard the rosemary sprigs. Stir in the cheeses and chopped parsley; mix well. Season to taste.

To Assemble

Divide the warm fennel among six warm, shallow bowls. Ladle about ½ cup (125 mL) of the lamb braising liquid over the fennel. Top each bowl with approximately ⅓ cup (175 mL) of the barley mixture. Place a lamb shank on top of the barley and sprinkle each serving with the reserved gremolata.

Roasted Sweetbreads on Potato-Onion Rösti with Braised Root Vegetables and Truffle Sauce

For 6 servings

Sweetbreads
2 lbs (1 kg) fresh veal sweetbreads
4 cups (1 L) milk
1 cup (250 mL) coarsely chopped white onion
1 cup (250 mL) peeled, coarsely chopped carrots
1 cup (250 mL) coarsely chopped celery
2 bay leaves
2 tsp (10 mL) whole black peppercorns
12 cups (3 L) water
1 tsp (5 mL) salt
2 tbsp (30 mL) canola oil
1/3 cup (75 mL) all-purpose flour (approx.)

Marinade
2 tbsp (30 mL) canola oil
1 clove garlic, minced
1 tbsp (15 mL) cracked black peppercorns
3 tbsp (45 mL) chopped parsley

Vegetables
8 oz (250 g) small carrots, peeled and halved
    lengthwise
8 oz (250 g) parsley root, peeled and
    halved lengthwise
1 tbsp (15 mL) butter
8 oz (250 g) small white turnips, peeled
    and halved
1 tsp (5 mL) minced garlic
1 bay leaf
1/2 cup (125 mL) chicken stock (see page 208)

Potato-Onion Rösti
2 1/2 lbs (1.25 kg) Yukon Gold potatoes,
    washed and scrubbed but not peeled
1 cup (250 mL) thinly sliced white onion
1/2 tsp (2 mL) caraway seeds
1 tsp (5 mL) salt
1/2 tsp (2 mL) freshly ground white pepper
1/4 tsp (1 mL) freshly grated nutmeg
1/3 cup (75 mL) canola oil
1/3 cup (75 mL) butter

Truffle Sauce
4 tsp (20 mL) cold butter, divided
1 tbsp (15 mL) chopped shallot
1 tsp (5 mL) cracked black peppercorns
1/2 tsp (2 mL) chopped garlic
1 tbsp (15 mL) brandy
1/2 cup (2 mL) red wine
4 cups (1 L) veal reduction (see page 210)
1 small bay leaf
1 tbsp (15 mL) chopped black winter truffle
    or truffle paste
1 tbsp (15 mL) Madeira or port wine
Salt

Garnish
Black truffles, sliced

Nose-to-tail

cooking is, in my opinion, important. If an animal is raised for food, it's disrespectful not to use every bit of it. And I've found that, if prepared with care, every part of an animal can be delicious. Sweetbreads, the thymus gland, and pancreas of a calf are a perfect example.

While sweetbreads have become more fashionable on restaurant menus during the last few years, I've been offering sweetbreads for more than 20 years and have customers who come to Pangaea hoping they'll be on the menu; however, sweetbreads perish quickly and, like fish, should be purchased only when very fresh. As a result, we buy only what we're sure we can sell, and that means we often run out on busy nights.

In my experience, the round pancreas is more delectable than the longer thymus. Regardless of which ones you find at the butcher's shop, choose the sweetbreads with the palest, pink-white colour. Then bring them home and prepare them as directed below.

This recipe uses a lot of milk that's later discarded, but brining the meat in milk is an essential part of the preparation process and ensures that the sweetbreads will be moist, sweet, and delicious. In the end, you'll have firm, creamy-textured meat that is a perfect partner for a rich, meaty glaze like the truffle sauce in this recipe.

Sweetbreads

Soak the sweetbreads in milk overnight. Drain and discard the milk. Rinse sweetbreads in cold water.

In a stockpot, combine the onions, carrots, celery, bay leaves, peppercorns, and sweetbreads. Fill the stockpot with the 12 cups (3 L) of cold water or enough to cover the sweetbreads by at least 1 inch (2.5 cm). Add the salt and bring to a boil; reduce heat and simmer for 2 minutes. Remove the sweetbreads; set on a tray and allow to cool enough to handle.

Find the edges of the membrane covering the sweetbreads and peel away, using your fingers. Trim away any gristle. Spread the cleaned sweetbreads on a clean tray or pan. Top with a second tray and a heavy weight. Transfer to the refrigerator and let stand for 2 hours or until the sweetbreads are well chilled. Discard any accumulated juices.

Marinade

Stir the oil with the garlic, cracked black pepper, and parsley. Place the sweetbreads into the marinade and toss to coat well. Reserve in the refrigerator for at least 30 minutes or for up to 12 hours.

Vegetables

Preheat the oven to 400°F (200°C). Cut the carrots and parsley root into 2-inch (5 cm) lengths.

Place a skillet over medium heat and add the butter. When the butter foams, add the parsley root, carrots, and turnips; toss to coat lightly. Stir in the garlic, bay leaf, and chicken stock; bring to a simmer. Cover skillet and place in the preheated oven for 20 minutes.

Remove cover; return skillet to stovetop and continue to simmer, stirring occasionally, until the liquids are reduced to a glaze and the vegetables are lightly browned around the edges. Taste and adjust seasoning if necessary. Keep warm.

Potato-Onion Rösti

Using the large holes on a box grater, grate the unpeeled potatoes into a large bowl.

Gather the grated potatoes with your hands and squeeze out and discard all the water you can. Toss in the onion, caraway seeds, salt, pepper, and nutmeg; mix well.

Heat 1 tablespoon (15 mL) each of the oil and butter in a small non-stick skillet set over medium heat. Divide the rösti mixture evenly into 6 portions. When the pan is very hot, add a portion of the potato mixture. Flatten and form into a disk using a spatula. Cook for 1 to 2 minutes without disturbing or until the underside is golden. Remove to a paper towel and keep warm on top of the stove or nearby. Repeat with the remaining oil, butter, and rösti mixture until you have 6 crisp, golden rösti.

Truffle Sauce

In a small saucepan set over medium-high heat, melt half the butter. Add the shallots and sauté until tender. Add the peppercorns and garlic and cook until the garlic begins to colour. Deglaze with brandy. Add the red wine and reduce until a thick, glossy syrup forms. Add the veal reduction and bay leaf and simmer until the sauce is thick enough to coat the back of a spoon. Pass the sauce through a fine-mesh strainer and return it to the stove. Add the chopped truffle and Madeira and bring to a gentle simmer. Whisk in the remaining cold butter, a little bit at a time. Remove from heat. Keep sauce warm.

To Assemble

Preheat the oven to 350°F (180°C). Heat the oil called for in the sweetbread recipe in a skillet set over medium heat. Remove the sweetbreads from the marinade; season on all sides with salt and dust with enough flour to coat. Brown, turning frequently, on all sides until evenly golden. Transfer the pan to the oven and roast for 15 minutes.

Arrange the vegetables in the centre of six warmed plates. Top with a rösti. Slice the sweetbreads and place several medallions on top of the rösti. Spoon sauce around the plate. Garnish the top with several slices of black truffle.

Rack

of pork, like rack of lamb, consists of the loin portion of the pork with the bones still attached. It's one of the choicest cuts. In beef, this cut is called "the prime rib," and it is just as tender and succulent when it's pork as when it's lamb or beef.

Pumpkin Seed Polenta offers an interesting twist on an Italian classic. We grate up handfuls of Monforte cloth-bound Cheddar (see page 85) and green pumpkin seeds that add distinctly Canadian flavour and crunch.

For 6 servings

Pork
1 six-bone rack of pork
1/2 tsp (2 mL) minced garlic
3/4 tsp (4 mL) minced jalapeño pepper
4 tsp (20 mL) chopped fresh thyme leaves
3 tbsp (45 mL) chopped fresh parsley
1 1/2 tsp (7 mL) coarsely ground black pepper
3 tbsp (45 mL) canola oil, divided
Salt to taste
2 tbsp (30 mL) pure maple syrup
Chervil or parsley sprigs

Mushrooms
2 tbsp (30 mL) butter (approx.)
12 king oyster mushrooms, about 1 lb
    (500 g), halved
1/4 cup (60 mL) white wine
1/2 tsp (2 mL) salt
1/4 tsp (1 mL) freshly ground black pepper

Pumpkin Seed Polenta
2 tbsp (30 mL) butter, divided
2 tbsp (30 mL) finely diced shallots
3 cups (750 mL) milk (approx.)
3/4 tsp (4 mL) salt
1/2 cup (125 mL) fine cornmeal
1/3 cup (75 mL) green pumpkin seeds
1 tsp (5 mL) chopped fresh thyme leaves
1 1/2 cups (375 mL) shredded aged
    Cheddar cheese

Lingonberry Sauce
1/2 stalk lemongrass
1 cup (250 mL) fresh or frozen lingonberries
1/4 cup (60 mL) red wine, such as Pinot Noir
1/4 cup (60 mL) granulated sugar
1 whole star anise
1 tsp (5 mL) grated fresh ginger
1/4 tsp (1 mL) ground cinnamon
1 1/2 cups (375 mL) veal reduction (see page 210)
Salt and freshly ground black pepper to taste

Pork
Divide the rack into 6 chops, each about 1 inch (2.5 cm) thick.

In a small bowl, combine the garlic, jalapeño, thyme, parsley, pepper, and 2 tbsp (30 mL) of the oil. Rub each chop thoroughly with the marinade. Cover tightly and refrigerate for at least 20 minutes or until ready to cook.

Mushrooms
In a skillet set over medium-high heat, melt the butter. When the butter begins to foam, add the mushrooms and sauté until golden. Deglaze the pan with white wine and season with salt and pepper. Keep warm.

Pumpkin Seed Polenta
In a large saucepan set over medium heat, melt half the butter. When the butter foams, add the shallots and sauté for 1 minute. Stir in the milk and salt, and heat until bubbles form around the edge of the saucepan. Watching constantly, bring to a boil. Immediately reduce the heat to medium-low and stir in the salt and cornmeal with a large whisk. Simmer, stirring occasionally, for 3 to 5 minutes or until thickened to the texture of cream of wheat. Stir in the pumpkin seeds and thyme. Stirring constantly, blend in the cheese until fully melted. Stir in the remaining butter and let polenta stand for 5 minutes. If too thick, adjust consistency by adding a little more warm milk.

Lingonberry Sauce
Place the lemongrass on a cutting board and flatten it with the back of a knife or a kitchen mallet. In a saucepan, combine lemongrass, berries, wine, sugar, star anise, ginger, and cinnamon. Bring to a simmer and cook for about 10 minutes or until the liquid is reduced by half. Remove and discard the lemongrass and star anise.

Heat the veal reduction in a saucepan set over medium heat. Add 2 tbsp (30 mL) of lingonberry mixture (reserve remaining lingonberry mixture to use as a condiment for other meats, such as game, turkey, and chicken). Simmer for 5 minutes; keep warm.

To Assemble
Preheat the oven to 375°F (190°C). Remove the pork from the marinade; shake off any excess and season with salt. Heat the remaining tablespoon (15 mL) of oil in a large skillet set over medium-high heat. Working in batches of 3 chops at a time, brown the chops for 2 minutes per side. Brush on both sides with maple syrup and transfer to a baking sheet lined with a wire rack. Bake for 5 to 7 minutes or until just pink in the centre. Let the chops rest for 5 minutes before serving.

Spoon a small amount of the Lingonberry Sauce in the centre of six warmed dinner plates. Divide the polenta and mushrooms among the plates. Lean a pork chop against the polenta, garnish the top with the chervil, and serve.

*The picture featured here shows this pork chop with green beans and the rosti featured on page 194.

Heritage Pork Chop
with Roasted King Oyster Mushrooms,
Pumpkin Seed Polenta, and
Lingonberry Sauce

Lingonberries
This recipe makes more Lingonberry Sauce then you'll need, but you can use it as a condiment for many different grilled or roasted meats and poultry.

If you can find fresh lingonberries, place them on a tray and check for any small rocks, moss, or stems, and rinse and dry well before use. If fresh berries are not available, frozen or preserved lingonberries will do. Just be sure to check for additives such as sugar. And if unsweetened frozen lingonberries aren't available, substitute fresh or frozen cranberries.

Tangy

desserts like this lemon tart are a wonderful way to end a filling winter meal. There's just nothing like it to re-awaken your palate and get your senses alert and ready for the cold.

For 8 servings

Meyer Lemon and Buttermilk Sherbet
2 cups (500 mL) granulated sugar
1 cup (250 mL) water
1/4 cup (60 mL) finely grated Meyer* lemon zest
1 1/4 cups (300 mL) Meyer* lemon juice
1 cup (250 mL) buttermilk

Crisp Poppy Seed Meringue
1/4 cup (60 mL) confectioners' (icing) sugar
1/4 cup (60 mL) granulated sugar, divided
1/4 cup (60 mL) egg whites, about 2, at
    room temperature
1 tbsp (15 mL) poppy seeds

Stewed Cranberries
1 cup (250 mL) fresh or thawed frozen
    cranberries
3/4 cup (175 mL) granulated sugar
3/4 cup (175 mL) water
1 tbsp (15 mL) freshly squeezed lemon juice

Pastry
1/3 cup (75 mL) cold butter, cubed
1/4 cup (60 mL) granulated sugar
1 egg, beaten
1/4 tsp (1 mL) vanilla extract
1 1/4 cups (300 mL) all-purpose flour
Pinch salt

Lemon Filling
1 cup (250 mL) granulated sugar
1/4 cup (60 mL) finely grated Meyer* lemon zest
4 eggs
1 cup (250 mL) freshly squeezed Meyer*
    lemon juice
1/3 cup (75 mL) cold unsalted butter, cubed

Garnish
1/2 cup (125 mL) chantilly cream
    (see page 213)

* Substitute regular lemons if necessary

As so often happens in the Pangaea kitchen, this recipe is a collaboration of sorts. The filling is adapted from one of my tried-and-true recipes, while the dough and garnishes are the handiwork of our pastry chef, Colen Quinn. Colen layers two tangy winter fruits — one local and one imported — to create a sensory experience that engages sight, smell, and taste in equal measure.

Meyer Lemon and Buttermilk Sherbet
Combine the sugar and water in a saucepan set over medium-high heat. Cook, stirring, until sugar is completely dissolved. Cool completely. Stir in the lemon zest and juice. Stir in the buttermilk. Chill completely.

Transfer to a chilled ice cream maker and proceed according to the manufacturer's instructions until mixture is thickened. Transfer to a tub that seals tightly and freeze until set enough to scoop.

(Alternatively, transfer the cooled mixture to a shallow, non-reactive pan; place in freezer. Stir occasionally with a whisk as crystals begin to form. Continue to freeze until the mixture is set and has formed a finely grainy texture.)

Crisp Poppy Seed Meringue
Line a 17- by 11-inch (43 by 28 cm) rimmed baking sheet with parchment paper. Preheat the oven to 200°F (100°C) and place a rack in the middle. Combine confectioners' sugar with 1 tbsp (15 mL) of the granulated sugar; reserve.

Using an electric mixer fitted with a whisk attachment, beat the egg whites on high speed until foamy. Add 1 tbsp (15 mL) of remaining granulated sugar and beat until mixture holds soft peaks. Gradually add the remaining granulated sugar while beating constantly until eggs form stiff, glossy peaks.

Gently fold the reserved icing sugar mixture and poppy seeds into the egg whites until evenly distributed.

Using a palette knife or a rubber spatula, spread the mixture onto the prepared pan in a very thin layer. Bake for 1 hour on the centre rack of the preheated oven, then turn off the heat and leave the pan in the warm oven for 20 minutes. Cool to room temperature. Break into shards and store in an airtight container.

Stewed Cranberries
Cut each cranberry into 3 or 4 equal slices. Combine the sugar, water, and lemon juice in a saucepan set over high heat. Bring to a boil. Add the cranberries and simmer for 2 to 3 minutes or until the liquid turns red and the cranberries are tender.

Pastry
In the bowl of an electric stand mixer fitted with a paddle attachment, beat the butter with the sugar on medium-high until light and fluffy; scrape down the bowl. Add the egg and vanilla and beat until well combined. Add the flour and salt and beat for 2 minutes on low speed, stopping to scrape down the bowl once, until the mixture is well combined.

Transfer the mixture to a clean surface and knead gently until the dough forms a smooth ball. Press into a disk and wrap tightly with plastic wrap. Chill for 2 hours or until firm.

Roll out dough on a clean work surface lightly dusted with flour. Using a 4-inch (10 cm) round cutter, cut out rounds. Set eight 3 1/2-inch (9 cm) tart rings on a parchment paper–lined baking sheet. Line each ring with a round of pastry that rises just above the top of the ring. Refrigerate for at least 30 minutes.

Preheat the oven to 350°F (180°C). Line each tart shell with parchment paper and pie weights. Bake for 20 minutes. Remove the weights, paper, and ring and cool slightly. Return to oven and bake for 15 minutes. Cool completely.

Lemon Tarts
with Stewed Cranberries, Meyer Lemon and Buttermilk Sherbet, Poppy Seed Meringue Shards, and Chantilly Cream

Lemon Filling

In a non-reactive, heatproof bowl or top of a double boiler, whisk the sugar with the lemon zest and eggs until well combined. Whisk in the lemon juice. Place the bowl over a saucepan filled with 1 inch (2.5 cm) of barely simmering water. Cook, whisking constantly, for 15 minutes or until the mixture is thickened. Pass the lemon mixture through a fine-mesh sieve. Add the butter, a few bits at a time, and stir until very smooth. Divide lemon mixture evenly into each tart shell. Refrigerate until set.

To Assemble

Set a lemon tart on the left side of eight large plates. Place a quenelle or dollop of chantilly cream on the other side of the plate and stand a few shards of poppy seed meringue up against it. At the front of the plate, just around the centre point, place a small scoop of sherbet. Spoon the stewed cranberries around the sherbet.

Tip

When using the zest of lemons — or any citrus fruit — it's important to choose organic fruit that has not been sprayed with pesticides or fertilizers and to wash the fruit well before zesting. The easiest way to zest citrus fruit is to use a hand-held zester or Microplane grater. Regardless of which tool you choose, be sure to remove only the colourful part of the peel and leave the white pith behind.

Surprised

best describes how I felt when I arrived at work early one morning to find pastry chef Colen Quinn opening a pint-sized can of Guinness. It's not that she's an abstainer; it's just that she had made it clear before that she's not a beer drinker.

I decided to play it cool and keep an eye on her. That first day, I noted that she used the beer (was it all of it? I can't say) to make the chocolate–stout ice cream in David Lebovitz's book *The Perfect Scoop*. In the afternoon, I noted that all the kitchen staff were sporting smiles. Then, the next morning, I saw her with another Guinness. This time, she was jotting notes and melting chocolate. Needless to say, I was curious.

By the end of the day, the mystery was solved when Colen invited me to try these wonderful milk chocolate–stout bars. "I don't like beer," she stated, "but it turns out that the rich, deep flavours in stout pair very well with milk chocolate." I took a bite and had to agree with her.

For 8 servings

Milk Chocolate–Stout Bar
$1/2$ cup (125 mL) stout beer such as Guinness
1 tsp (5 mL) powdered gelatin
$4^1/2$ oz (135 g) pure milk baking chocolate
$3/4$ cup (175 mL) whipping (35%) cream

Chocolate Tumbleweed
2 oz (60 g) bittersweet chocolate
Ice cubes

Soufflé
8 oz (250 g) good-quality dark chocolate
1 tbsp (15 mL) butter
$1/3$ cup (75 mL) homogenized milk
3 egg yolks
4 egg whites
Pinch cream of tartar
$1/3$ cup (75 mL) granulated sugar
Cocoa powder

Milk Chocolate–Stout Bar

Measure out 2 tbsp (30 mL) of the beer and place in a small bowl. Sprinkle over the gelatin and let stand for 5 minutes. Place a mixing bowl in the freezer. Line a 9- by 5-inch (23 by 12.5 cm) loaf pan with a piece of parchment paper that is long enough to overlap the ends of the pan but only as wide as the bottom of the pan.

Meanwhile, chop the milk chocolate and place in a metal bowl or top of a double boiler. Add the remaining beer. Set bowl over a saucepan of barely simmering water and heat, stirring often, until the chocolate is completely melted. Remove pan from heat. Set the gelatin mixture over the boiling water and heat until liquefied. Add the gelatin mixture to warm chocolate and stir with rubber spatula until the mixture is smooth. Cool to body temperature.

Place the cream in the chilled mixing bowl. Using an electric mixer or a whisk, whip cream until soft peaks form. Fold into the chocolate mixture. Spoon mixture into the prepared loaf pan. Smooth the top and place in the freezer for 2 to 3 hours or until set. Using the ends of the parchment paper as handles, lift the bar out onto a cutting board. Cut crosswise into 8 bars. (Bars can be made to this point, loosely wrapped, and reserved in the freezer for up to 5 days.)

Chocolate Tumbleweed

Place two rimmed baking trays and a small offset palette knife in the freezer. Line a plate with parchment or waxed paper and place in the refrigerator.

Chop the bittersweet chocolate and place in a clean metal bowl. Set over a saucepan of barely simmering water and cook, stirring often, until completely melted. Remove pan from heat.

Make a paper cone: Cut an 8- by 14-inch (20 by 45 cm) piece of parchment paper. Fold this rectangle in half diagonally and cut along the fold. Fold the short side of one triangle over to the right-angled corner to form a cone. (Reserve the other triangle for use another time.) Holding the cone together with one hand, wrap the long, pointed, tail end of the triangle around the paper cone. Tuck the loose point of the paper inside the cone to secure it.

Use a small rubber spatula to scrape the melted chocolate into the cone. Fold over the top to enclose the chocolate in the cone. Cut a small snip in the tip of the cone to allow the chocolate to drizzle out in a thin stream when the cone is gently squeezed.

Remove one of the rimmed baking trays from the freezer. Fill with ice. Place the other baking tray over the ice, bottom side facing up. Working to make one at a time, drizzle about 20 fine lines of chocolate onto the pan to make a loose rectangle about 7 inches (17.5 cm) long and $1^1/4$ inches (3 cm) wide. Just as the chocolate begins to lose its gloss, place the chilled palette knife at the short end of the piped chocolate so that the blade is at a 90-degree angle to the pan. Moving very quickly, pull the palette knife toward you so that the chocolate curls up into a circular shape. Immediately transfer the tumbleweed

Warm Dark Chocolate Soufflé
with Crème Anglaise, Frozen Milk Chocolate–Stout Bar,
and Chocolate Tumbleweed

very gently to the refrigerator. Reserve for up to 2 hours. Repeat to make 10 or 12 portions (you'll need a few extras, since this garnish is very fragile and breaks very easily).

Soufflé

Cut 8 pieces of parchment paper, each 10 inches (25 cm) long by 1½ inches (4 cm) wide. Place 8 pastry rings, each 3¼ inches (8 cm) wide and ¾ inch (2 cm) tall, on a parchment paper–lined baking sheet. Line each ring with a strip of parchment paper so that the paper goes around the circumference of the ring and stands about 1 inch (2.5 cm) above the ring's rim. (Alternatively, butter eight 6-oz (175 mL) ramekins and set on a baking sheet.)

Chop the dark chocolate and place in a heatproof bowl. Add the butter and milk and place over a saucepan of barely simmering water. Melt, stirring often, until liquefied. Remove from heat and cool to body temperature. Stir in the egg yolks until smooth, thick, and glossy.

In the bowl of an electric stand mixer fitted with the whisk attachment, combine the egg whites with the cream of tartar and beat until foamy. Gradually add the sugar and continue to whip until stiff peaks form. Fold half the egg whites into the chocolate mixture until streaky. Add the remaining egg whites and fold until well combined. Spoon the batter into the parchment paper–lined rings or buttered ramekins. (Soufflés can be prepared to this point and refrigerated for up to 1½ hours.)

To Assemble

Preheat the oven to 425°F (220°C). Bake soufflés for 10 minutes or until risen and lightly set.

Meanwhile, spread out eight rectangular dessert plates. Using a squeeze bottle, pipe a line of crème anglaise (see page 213) down the centre of the plate. On the right side of this line, sprinkle a little cocoa powder and icing sugar; place a Milk Chocolate–Stout Bar. Top with a piece of Chocolate Tumbleweed.

Remove the soufflés from oven and dust with cocoa powder. Carefully run a knife around the edge of the soufflé to release from the paper and use an offset palette knife to lift onto serving plates. (If using ramekins, place each baking dish on a serving plate.) Serve immediately.

My love

of banana cream and coconut cream pies began in 1987 when I met pastry icon Jim Dodge when he visited Toronto on his book tour for *The American Baker*. (I still have my signed copy of his book and use it often at home.)

Pastry

½ cup (125 mL) cold butter, cubed
¼ cup (60 mL) granulated sugar
1 egg yolk
2 tbsp (30 mL) whipping (35%) cream
1½ cups (375 mL) all-purpose flour (approx.)
Pinch salt

Coconut Pastry Cream

½ cup (125 mL) toasted (see tip page 203), sweetened, shredded coconut
3 cups (750 mL) whole (homogenized) milk (approx.)
¼ tsp (1 mL) vanilla extract
1½ cups (375 mL) sweetened, shredded coconut
6 tbsp (90 mL) granulated sugar, divided
2 tbsp (30 mL) all-purpose flour
3 eggs
6 tbsp (90 mL) cold, butter, cubed
2 bananas

Toasted Coconut Sherbet

3 cups (750 mL) whole (homogenized) milk
⅓ cup (75 mL) granulated sugar
1½ cups (375 mL) toasted, sweetened, shredded coconut, divided
¼ tsp (1 mL) vanilla extract

Caramelized Bananas

2 bananas, peeled
½ cup (125 mL) granulated sugar (approx.)

Mango Purée

1 ripe mango, peeled and cut into chunks
2 tbsp (30 mL) granulated sugar

Garnish

½ cup (125 mL) chantilly cream (see page 213)
1 cup (250 mL) white chocolate shards

Pangaea's dessert menu featured a single-serve version of Jim's two recipes combined as banana–coconut cream pie when the restaurant first opened and we couldn't afford a full-fledged pastry chef. Later, when Joanne Yolles joined our team, she finessed our banana–coconut cream pie by adding her signature touches, and customers swooned.

Today, our present pastry chef, Colen Quinn, has modified the recipe yet again and made it even more wonderful by toasting coconut to infuse flavour into the pastry cream. As a result, this dessert, like Pangaea itself, just keeps getting better with time.

Pastry

In the bowl of an electric stand mixer fitted with a paddle attachment, blend the butter and sugar on medium speed for 1 minute or until the ingredients are well combined. With a whisk, blend the egg yolk with the cream. Add to the butter mixture and mix until incorporated. Scrape down the sides of the bowl with a rubber spatula. Add the flour and salt and mix on low speed for 1 minute or until a dough forms.

Transfer to a clean work surface lightly dusted with flour and knead gently into a smooth ball. Flatten into a disk and wrap tightly. Chill for 2 hours or until firm.

Roll out dough on a clean work surface lightly dusted with flour. Using a 4-inch (10 cm) round cutter, cut out rounds. Set eight 3½-inch (9 cm) tart rings on a parchment paper–lined baking sheet. Line each ring with a round of pastry that is just slightly higher than the top of the ring. Refrigerate for at least 30 minutes.

Preheat the oven to 350°F (180°C). Line each tart shell with parchment paper and pie weights. Bake for 20 minutes. Remove the weights, paper, and ring and cool slightly. Return to oven and bake for 15 minutes. Cool completely.

Coconut Pastry Cream

In a large saucepan, combine the toasted coconut, milk, and vanilla. Place over medium-high heat and heat just until mixture comes to a boil. Reduce heat to low and simmer for 10 minutes.

Strain milk into a clean saucepan and discard coconut. You should have 2½ cups (625 mL) of infused milk; add additional milk if necessary to reach this amount. Add the untoasted coconut and half the sugar. Bring to a boil and simmer gently for 10 minutes. Remove from the heat.

In a bowl, combine the remaining sugar, flour, and eggs, whisking until smooth. Pour a little of the milk mixture into the bowl and whisk well. Transfer all of the egg mixture to the saucepan, scraping every bit into the pan with a rubber spatula. Return pan to heat. Cook, stirring constantly, over medium heat, for 5 minutes. Remove from heat and whisk in butter. Cool to room temperature. Cover tightly and refrigerate until well chilled.

Toasted Coconut Sherbet

Combine the milk, sugar, and 1 cup (250 mL) of the toasted coconut in a large saucepan. Bring to a boil, then reduce the heat to very low and simmer for 1 hour, stirring all the way to the bottom of the pan every 10 minutes or so. Strain and discard the solids. Stir in vanilla and cool to room temperature. Cover tightly and refrigerate overnight.

Transfer the chilled mixture to an ice cream machine and churn according to manufacturer's instructions. Transfer to a tub that

Banana–Coconut Cream Pie with White Chocolate, Mango Purée, Toasted Coconut Sherbet, and Caramelized Bananas

seals tightly and freeze until set enough to scoop. Just before serving, make 8 small scoops of ice cream. Spread remaining toasted coconut on a plate and roll each scoop in coconut. Transfer to a parchment paper–lined plate and freeze for 5 to 10 minutes or until set.

Caramelized Bananas

Slice the bananas on the bias into 24 thin slices, each about ¹/₄ inch (6 mm) thick. Lay on a rack set over a parchment paper–lined metal baking tray. Sprinkle evenly with sugar. Using a blowtorch, melt the sugar covering the bananas until amber. Cool just long enough for sugar to solidify into a hard, clear caramel.

Mango Purée

Combine the mango and sugar in a blender. Purée, adding up to 2 tbsp (30 mL) water if necessary, until mixture is smooth and thin enough to drizzle through the tip of a squeeze bottle. Makes approximately ²/₃ cup (150 mL).

To Assemble

Peel the 2 bananas listed under the pastry cream and slice thinly into 24 pieces. On a large plate (you'll need eight), place a baked tart shell. Arrange 3 banana slices in the bottom of each shell. Divide the pastry cream evenly among the shells, mounding it up in the middle. Place the chantilly cream in a piping bag fitted with a round tip; pipe circles of cream all over each tart. Garnish with long shards of white chocolate.

Using a squeeze bottle, make an archipelago of mango purée dots in an arc around the outside of the tart. Place a scoop of coconut-rolled ice cream on each plate, and in the remaining space, arrange 3 caramelized banana slices.

Tip

To toast coconut, preheat the oven to 375°F (190°C). Spread the coconut in a thin, even layer on a rimmed baking sheet. Bake for 5 to 6 minutes, stirring once or twice, until well browned. Cool completely. (Coconut can be toasted, cooled, and reserved in an airtight container for up to 1 week.)

Basics

Basics

Stocks and Reductions

Vegetable Preparations

Savoury Preparations

Sweet Preparations

Savoury Sauces

Sweet Sauces and Toppings

Stocks and Reductions

Chicken Stock

2 tbsp (30 mL) canola oil
1 cup (250 mL) chopped carrot
1 cup (250 mL) chopped celery
1 cup (250 mL) chopped onion
1 cup (250 mL) white wine
6 lbs (3 kg) chicken bones
1 tbsp (15 mL) whole black peppercorns
3 cloves garlic
2 bay leaves

Heat the oil in a large stockpot (at least 60 cups/14 L) set over medium heat. Add the carrots, celery, and onions and cook, covered but stirring occasionally, for 5 minutes. Add the wine and cook, covered, for 1 minute. Add the bones, peppercorns, garlic, and bay leaves. Top with 32 cups (8 L) of cold water.

Bring to a boil and cook for 20 minutes. Reduce heat and skim scum from top of broth and discard. Simmer for 2 ½ hours; cool slightly.

Using tongs, remove the large bones from the pot and discard. Strain the broth into another large pot or a heatproof container. Discard all solids. Makes 24 cups (6 L).

Double Chicken Stock

2 tbsp (30 mL) canola oil
1 cup (250 mL) chopped carrot
1 cup (250 mL) chopped celery
1 cup (250 mL) chopped onion
1 cup (250 mL) white wine
6 lbs (3 kg) chicken bones
1 tbsp (15 mL) whole black peppercorns
3 cloves garlic
2 bay leaves
24 cups (6 L) cold chicken stock

Heat the oil in a large stockpot (at least 60 cups/14 L) set over medium heat. Add the carrots, celery, and onions and cook, covered but stirring occasionally, for 5 minutes. Add the wine and cook, covered, for 1 minute. Add the bones, peppercorns, garlic, and bay leaves. Top with cold chicken stock.

Bring to a boil; reduce heat to a simmer and skim scum from top of broth and discard. Simmer, uncovered, for 2 ½ hours, adding more water as necessary to maintain the original volume; cool slightly.

Using tongs, remove the large bones from the pot and discard. Strain the broth into another large pot or a heatproof container. Discard all solids. Makes 24 cups (6 L).

Dark Chicken Stock

2 lbs (1 kg) chicken bones chopped, fat discarded
1 tbsp (15 mL) canola oil
1 cup (250 mL) diced onion
1 cup (250 mL) diced carrot
1 cup (250 mL) diced celery
1 cup (250 mL) red wine
1 bay leaf
1 tsp (5 mL) whole black peppercorns

Preheat the oven to 375°F (190°C). Place chicken bones and oil in a large skillet set over high heat. Cook, turning the bones frequently, for 10 minutes or until well browned. Add the onions, carrots, and celery and sauté for 2 minutes. Transfer the skillet to the oven and roast for 40 minutes.

Transfer the skillet back to the stovetop and set over medium-high heat. Deglaze the pan with red wine and simmer gently for 20 minutes or until the wine is reduced by about 50%.

Transfer the bones, vegetables, and all the accumulated juices to a Dutch oven. Add 5 cups (1.25 L) of cold water, the bay leaf, and the peppercorns to the pan. Bring to a boil; reduce the heat to low. Simmer for 4 hours, adding more water as necessary to maintain the original depth. Cool slightly and skim the fat from the top. Strain the stock and discard the solids. Makes 5 cups (1.25 L).

Dark Chicken Reduction

1 tbsp (15 mL) butter
2 tbsp (30 mL) chopped shallots
$\frac{1}{2}$ tsp (2 mL) coarsely ground black pepper
   or to taste
1 bay leaf
1 clove garlic, minced
1 cup (250 mL) red wine
5 cups (1.25 L) dark chicken stock
$\frac{1}{4}$ tsp (1 mL) finely chopped fresh
   thyme leaves
Salt to taste
1 tsp (5 mL) cold diced butter

In a large saucepan set over medium-high heat, melt the butter until it begins to foam. Add the chopped shallots, pepper, and bay leaf. Sauté for 1 minute or until the shallots are golden. Stir in the garlic and cook for 30 seconds.

Deglaze with the red wine and simmer for 20 minutes or until the liquid is reduced by about half of the original volume of wine. Add the dark chicken stock; bring to a boil. Reduce heat to low and simmer, skimming any foam that develops from the top, for 2 hours or until the sauce is thick enough to coat the back of a spoon.

Strain through a fine sieve, pressing the solids down with the back of a ladle or a spoon to remove all the fluid. Stir the thyme into the sauce; taste and season with salt and additional pepper if necessary. (Sauce can be made to this point up to 3 days ahead and reheated just before use.) Reheat the sauce until hot; remove from heat and whisk in the bits of butter. Makes $\frac{1}{3}$ cup (75 mL).

Fish Fumet

Select bones from non-oily fish such as flounder, sole, halibut, turbot, and plaice. Remove any veins along the inside of the rib cage by rubbing them with your fingertips under cold running water.

4 lbs (2 kg) fish bones, heads and tails
   removed
1 tbsp (15 mL) canola oil
$\frac{1}{2}$ cup (125 mL) diced fennel
$\frac{1}{2}$ cup (125 mL) diced celery
$\frac{1}{2}$ cup (125 mL) diced onion
$\frac{1}{2}$ cup (125 mL) white wine
1 tbsp (15 mL) whole black peppercorns
3 cloves garlic
2 bay leaves
3 sprigs fresh thyme
3 sprigs fresh parsley
1 tsp (5 mL) kosher salt

Chop the fish bones into 4-inch (10 cm) lengths; rinse under cold running water. Drain well. Heat the oil in a large stockpot set over medium heat. Add the fennel, celery, and onions; cook, covered but stirring occasionally, for 2 minutes. Add the wine and reduce to a glaze. Add 10 cups (2.5 L) of cold water along with the fish bones, peppercorns, garlic, bay leaves, thyme, parsley, and salt. (Add more water if necessary to cover the fish bones.) Bring to a simmer without allowing it to come to a rolling boil and cook, uncovered, for 30 minutes. Skim off any scum that accumulates at the top.

Remove from heat and set aside for 10 minutes to allow all the solids to settle to the bottom of the pot. Ladle out the fumet, taking care not to disturb the solids, and pass through a chinois. Cool to room temperature and then refrigerate in a clean, dry container. Makes approximately 8 cups (2 L).

Rabbit Stock

2 lbs (1 kg) rabbit bones, chopped
1 tbsp (15 mL) canola oil
1 cup (250 mL) diced onion
1 cup (250 mL) diced carrot
1 cup (250 mL) diced celery
1 cup (250 mL) red wine
1 bay leaf
1 tsp (5 mL) whole black peppercorns

Preheat the oven to 375°F (190°C). Place rabbit bones and oil in a large skillet set over high heat. Sauté, turning the bones frequently, for 10 minutes or until well browned. Add the onions, carrots, and celery and sauté for 2 minutes. Transfer the skillet to the oven and roast for 40 minutes.

Transfer the skillet back to the stovetop and set over medium-high heat. Deglaze the pan with red wine and simmer gently for 20 minutes or until the volume of wine is reduced by about 50%.

Transfer the bones, vegetables, and all the accumulated juices to a Dutch oven. Add 5 cups (1.25 L) of cold water, the bay leaf, and the peppercorns to the pan. Bring to a boil, then reduce the heat to low. Simmer for 4 hours, adding more water as necessary to maintain the original depth. Cool slightly and skim the fat from the top. Strain the stock and discard the solids. Makes 5 cups (1.25 L).

Rabbit Reduction

1 tbsp (15 mL) butter
2 tbsp (30 mL) chopped shallots
$^{1}/_{2}$ tsp (2 mL) coarsely ground black pepper
    (approx.)
1 bay leaf
1 clove garlic, minced
1 cup (250 mL) red wine
5 cups (1.25 L) rabbit stock
$^{1}/_{4}$ tsp (1 mL) finely chopped fresh
    rosemary leaves
Salt and freshly ground black pepper
1 tsp (5 mL) cold diced butter

In a large saucepan set over medium-high heat, melt the butter until it begins to foam. Add the shallots, pepper, and bay leaf. Sauté for 1 minute or until the shallots are golden. Stir in the garlic and cook for 30 seconds. Deglaze with the red wine and simmer for 20 minutes or until the wine is reduced by about half.

Add the rabbit stock; bring to a boil. Reduce heat to low and simmer, uncovered, skimming any scum that accumulates at the top, for 2 hours or until the sauce is thick enough to coat the back of a spoon.

Strain through a fine sieve, pressing the solids down with the back of a ladle or a spoon to remove all the fluid. Stir in the rosemary; taste and season with salt and additional pepper if necessary. (Sauce can be made to this point up to 3 days ahead and reheated just before use.)

Reheat the sauce until hot; remove from heat and whisk in the bits of butter. Makes approximately $^{1}/_{3}$ cup (75 mL)

Veal Stock

5 lbs (2.5 kg) veal bones
2 cups (500 mL) red wine, divided
2 tbsp (30 mL) canola oil
1 cup (250 mL) diced onion
1 cup (250 mL) diced carrot
1 cup (250 mL) diced celery
$^{3}/_{4}$ cup (175 mL) tomato paste
1 bay leaf
2 cloves garlic
5 sprigs fresh thyme
5 sprigs fresh parsley
1 tsp (5 mL) whole black peppercorns

Preheat the oven to 375°F (190°C). Arrange veal bones in a single layer in a roasting pan; place on the middle oven rack. Roast for 1 hour, turning the bones every 15 minutes to brown evenly.

Remove roasting pan from the oven. Remove the bones, drain off the accumulated fat, and deglaze with half the wine, scraping the bottom of the roasting pan clean.

Meanwhile, in a large stockpot set over medium-high heat, heat the oil. Add the onions, carrots, and celery and cook for 15 minutes or until the edges of the vegetables begin to soften and colour. Stir in the tomato paste and cook until it browns, scraping the bottom of the pan occasionally to prevent scorching. Add the rest of the red wine, the veal bones, and the roasting glaze to the stockpot. Add twice the volume of cold water to bones. Stir in the bay leaf, garlic, thyme, parsley, and peppercorns.

Bring to a boil, reduce to a simmer, and cook for 4 to 6 hours, skimming the scum as it accumulates on top of the liquid. Add more water as necessary to maintain the original volume. Strain the stock and discard the solids. Makes about 10 cups (2.5 L).

Veal Reduction

1 tbsp (15 mL) butter
2 tbsp (30 mL) chopped shallots
$^{1}/_{2}$ tsp (2 mL) coarsely ground black pepper
1 small bay leaf
2 cloves garlic, minced
2 cups (500 mL) red wine
10 cups (2.5 L) veal stock
$^{1}/_{2}$ tsp (2 mL) chopped fresh sage leaves
Salt to taste
2 tsp (10 mL) cold diced butter

In a large Dutch oven set over medium-high heat, melt the butter until it begins to foam. Add the shallots, pepper, and bay leaf. Sauté for 1 minute or until the shallots are golden. Stir in the garlic and cook for 30 seconds. Deglaze the pan with the red wine and simmer for 20 minutes or until the wine is reduced by about half.

Add the veal stock; bring to a boil. Reduce the heat to low and simmer, skimming any foam that develops from the top, for 4 hours or until the sauce is thick enough to coat the back of a spoon.

Strain through a fine sieve, pressing the solids down with the back of a ladle or a spoon to remove all the fluid. Stir in the sage; taste and season with salt and additional pepper if necessary. (Sauce can be made to this point, cooled, transferred to a clean, dry container, and refrigerated for up to 3 days ahead. Reheat just before use.)

Reheat the sauce until hot; remove from heat and whisk in the bits of butter, one piece at a time. Makes approximately 1 cup (250 mL).

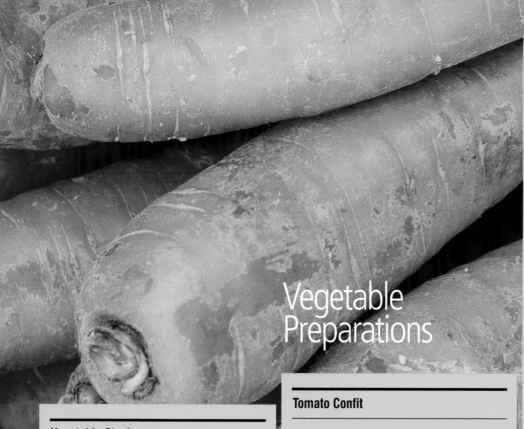

Vegetable Preparations

Vegetable Stock

2 tbsp (30 mL) canola oil
1 cup (250 mL) diced fennel
1 cup (250 mL) diced carrot
1 cup (250 mL) thinly sliced leek, white only, rinsed well
$^1/_2$ cup (125 mL) white wine
1 tbsp (15 mL) whole black peppercorns
2 bay leaves
5 sprigs fresh thyme
10 sprigs fresh parsley
1 tsp (5 mL) kosher salt

Heat the oil in a large stockpot set over medium heat. Add the fennel, carrots, and leek. Cook, covered but stirring occasionally, for 5 minutes. Add the wine and simmer to a glaze.

Add enough water to cover all the vegetables. Toss in the peppercorns, bay leaves, thyme, parsley, and salt. Bring to a boil, then reduce heat and simmer for 45 minutes. Skim off any scum that accumulates at the top. Remove from heat and strain into a clean, dry container. Discard solids. Makes approximately 4 cups (1 L).

Tomato Confit

6 plum (Roma) tomatoes
2 tbsp (30 mL) extra virgin olive oil
$^1/_4$ tsp (1 mL) kosher salt
Pinch freshly ground black pepper

Preheat the oven to 230°F (110°C). Using a sharp knife, score the bottom of each tomato with a small X. Blanch the tomatoes for 20 seconds in a saucepan of boiling water; immediately drain and plunge into ice water. Once the tomatoes are cool enough to handle, peel off the skin. Quarter tomatoes lengthwise and remove the seeds. Pat the tomato pieces dry and toss in a bowl with olive oil, salt, and pepper.

Line a rimmed baking sheet with parchment paper and spread the tomatoes out cut-side up. Bake in the preheated oven for 2$^1/_2$ to 3 hours or until tomato pieces have shrunk to half their original size.

Remove the tray from the oven and cool to room temperature. Place the tomatoes in a storage container with a tight-fitting lid; pour any liquid that accumulated in the tray during cooking overtop. Cover and refrigerate until ready for use.

Cooked and Marinated Artichokes

We wait until the artichokes are at the right size, small but before the thistle (choke) begins to form inside, and then purchase several cases at a time.

This is a tough job, and the entire kitchen gets involved to plow through them quickly.

Marinade

1 cup (250 mL) white wine vinegar
4 cups (1 L) extra virgin olive oil

Artichokes

2 tbsp (30 mL) freshly squeezed lemon juice or vitamin C powder (approx.)
2 tsp kosher salt
18 small artichokes

Marinade

In a large bowl, combine the white wine vinegar, and olive oil and set aside.

Artichokes

Fill a large saucepan with about 6 cups (1.5 L) cold water and add the lemon juice and salt. Taste and add more lemon juice if necessary to make the water taste decidedly lemony.

Peel away the tough outer leaves until you reach the tender pale green leaves and the artichoke is bullet-shaped. Cut off the tops and trim the perimeter of the artichoke where the leaves were. Peel and trim the stem of the artichoke, keeping the shape intact, and submerge in the acidulated water. Fit a clean tea towel over the artichokes to prevent exposure to air.

Place the saucepan over high heat; bring to a boil, then reduce to a simmer. Cook the artichokes for 15 to 20 minutes or until just tender. Remove from the heat and drain well.

When the artichokes are cool enough to handle, cut each one in half lengthwise. Don't worry about any discolouration inside; this will fade over time once immersed in the marinade. Gently toss the artichokes with the marinade. Place the artichokes in a storage container with a tight-fitting lid and pour the marinade overtop. Refrigerate for 3 days before using.

Savoury Preparations

Roasted Garlic

1 tbsp (15 mL) butter
12 cloves garlic
³/₄ cup (175 mL) chicken stock (see page 208)
    or water

In a small skillet set over medium heat, heat the butter. Add the garlic cloves and cook, stirring often, for 5 minutes or until well browned all over. Add the stock and bring to a boil. Cover the pan tightly and simmer for 5 to 10 minutes or until the garlic is very soft and all the liquid is evaporated. Cool to room temperature.

Pickled Ginger

1 cup (250 mL) rice wine vinegar
1 cup (250 mL) granulated sugar
1 lb (500 g) fresh ginger

Combine the vinegar and sugar and bring to a boil. Remove from heat; cool completely.

Meanwhile, peel the ginger using a vegetable peeler or the edge of a spoon. Discard peels. Slice the ginger into long, paper-thin tendrils using a mandoline.

Bring a saucepan of water to a boil. Blanch the sliced ginger in the boiling water for approximately 1 minute; drain and transfer to an ice bath until cool. Strain the ginger and pat dry. Transfer to a shallow dish. Pour over the reserved vinegar syrup. Cover tightly. Let stand in the refrigerator for at least 24 hours before use. Ginger can be reserved in syrup for up to 2 months. (If keeping for longer than a few days, transfer to a sterilized jar with a tight-fitting lid.) Makes about 3 cups (750 mL).

Sweet Preparations

Crisp Candied Ginger

1 large piece fresh ginger
1 cup (250 mL) granulated sugar
1 cup (250 mL) water
Oil for deep-frying

Peel and slice the ginger lengthwise into paper-thin pieces using a vegetable peeler or mandoline. Combine the sugar and water and bring to a boil; add the ginger. Boil for 10 minutes. Remove from the heat and leave the ginger to cool and steep in the syrup for 1 day.

Remove the ginger from syrup; pat dry on paper towels. Following manufacturer's instructions, fill a deep-fryer with oil. Heat to 300°F (150°C); add the dried ginger slices, working in batches if necessary, and fry until crisp and just golden brown. Drain on paper towel.

Savoury Sauces

Butter Sauce

1 cup (250 mL) cold butter, cut
   into small cubes, divided
1 tsp (5 mL) minced shallot
$^1/_2$ tsp (2 mL) minced garlic
1 cup (250 mL) white wine
2 tbsp (30 mL) freshly squeezed lemon juice
$^1/_4$ cup (50 mL) whipping (35%) cream
Pinch cayenne pepper
Salt and freshly ground white pepper

In a small saucepan set over medium heat,
melt 1 tsp (5 mL) of the butter. Once it foams,
stir in the shallots and garlic and heat until
fragrant, about 45 seconds. Add the white
wine and lemon juice. Bring to a boil; reduce
the heat and simmer until the liquid is
reduced by three-quarters. Add the cream
and reduce by half. Reduce the heat to low
and whisk in all the butter, adding cubes one
at a time and fully incorporating each
piece before adding the next. Remove from
heat and stain through a fine sieve into
a clean, dry stainless steel or glass container.
Add cayenne and season to taste with salt
and pepper. Keep warm for up to 30 minutes
or until ready to use. Makes approximately
1 cup (250 mL).

Sweet Sauces and Toppings

Chantilly Cream

2 cups (500 mL) cold whipping (35%) cream
2 tbsp (30 mL) confectioners' (icing) sugar
1 tsp (5 mL) vanilla extract

Place a mixing bowl and a set of electric
beaters in the freezer and chill completely.
Place the cold cream in the cold bowl
and whip on medium speed until frothy and
beginning to thicken. Add the confectioners'
sugar and vanilla and increase speed to high.
Whip until cream is thick and stiff enough
to hold its shape when spooned out onto
a plate. Keep cold. Make up to 1 hour before
using. Recipe halves and doubles easily.

Vanilla Crème Anglaise

1 vanilla bean
1 cup (250 mL) whipping (35%) cream
1 cup (250 mL) whole (homogenized) milk
$^1/_3$ cup (75 mL) granulated sugar, divided
5 egg yolks

Halve the vanilla bean lengthwise. Set aside
one half for another use. Using a sharp knife,
scrape the seeds from the remaining half.
Place the scraped beans, cream, milk, and
half the sugar in a small saucepan. Place over
medium-high heat and bring just to a boil;
remove pan from heat.

In a bowl, whisk the remaining sugar with
the egg yolks. Pour a little of the hot
cream mixture into the egg mixture and
whisk well. Scrape all the egg mixture into
the saucepan and return to stove. Cook,
whisking constantly, until the mixture coats
the back of a spoon. Strain into a clean,
dry squeeze bottle or other container and
cool completely. Cover tightly and refrigerate
for up to 5 days. Makes 2 cups (500 mL).

Index

Acknowledgements

So many people helped to make this book something I'm proud of that it would take pages to mention them all by name. First off, thanks to Pangaea's patrons, who for 14 years have supported us with their business, allowing Peter and I to fulfil our professional dreams at 1221 Bay Street.

Next, thanks to our staff — many of whom have worked for us for more than a decade. On an hourly basis, these men and women make the words in this book come to life. I truly admire and appreciate their dedication to excellence and thank each of them for choosing Pangaea as their professional home.

Our suppliers deserve the most credit for making this book possible, from the people mentioned on these pages to the many others, such as Ronald Francis, who not only provides Pangaea with spectacular tea but also travels to Ceylon to personally supervise the harvest of the tea leaves. Likewise, Wolf Kraus, our small-wares supplier and full-time friend, is a behind-the-scenes contributor to this book. He gave us full access to his dish collection so we had plenty of props when we were taking the food pictures in this book. And there are dozens more stories and people I could introduce if I had more pages.

Thanks also to our creative team and their extended teams. I've learned so much about photography, writing, recipe testing, food styling, and book creation during this process, and it's because each of you shared your expertise.

And, last, thanks to my business partner, Peter Geary, who tolerated my frequent absences and distractions while this book was being written.

Martin Kouprie
Autumn 2010

Our Creative Team

Martin Kouprie

Ask chef Martin Kouprie the secret of his culinary success and he'll tell you that it's a love of fresh food. In fact, fresh ingredients get Martin Kouprie's creative juices running high. "One of the most amazing recent experiences I've had was harvesting U-10–sized divers' scallops with my own hands in the icy waters off Newfoundland," explains Martin. "I couldn't resist sampling a few of those gorgeous fresh scallops right from their shells when I got back on the boat. Once you know what truly fresh food tastes like, you'll never compromise your cooking by using less-than-perfect ingredients."

This passion for freshness and an understanding of the science of cooking allow Martin to create menus and recipes that celebrate the magnificence of each season's harvest. Although local ingredients hold centre stage in Martin's cooking, he also views his pantry through the lens of the latest food trends. As a result, Martin's fans come to Pangaea to enjoy his ingredient-driven cooking, which is simultaneously regional, modern, and sophisticated. This is Martin's first book.

Read Martin's companion blog to this book at http://seasonedtoperfection.wordpress.com.

Peter Geary

The service at Pangaea is warm, competent, and thoughtful but never pretentious — a reflection of Peter's personal style. "I like to think of Pangaea as an extension of my home," he says. "By the time one of our guests is seated, they should feel confident that they're in good hands."

Highly respected as an industry leader, Peter has been a guest lecturer at Humber College on the subject of service.

For more information or to contact Peter, visit www.pangaearestaurant.com.

Colen Quinn

A childhood love of baking became a passion for Colen and led her to the top of her class when she was a baking and patisserie apprentice at Toronto's George Brown College. Now, as pastry chef at Pangaea, her goal is to use seasonal and regional ingredients to keep the Pangaea dessert menu fresh and satisfying all year long.

While working on this book, Colen left her cozy pastry nook at Pangaea to work in a professional test kitchen, where she personally supervised the testing and writing of every dessert recipe in this book. "I think chocolate desserts are sometimes over-rated, so I rarely order them when I go out for dinner. As a result, I made sure the chocolate dessert I included in this book is special and worth every calorie," admits Pangaea's Queen of Tarts.

John Speakman

John Speakman is one of Canada's leading art directors. During a 40-year career he has produced notable advertising for many clients, including Molson, Labatts, Amstel, Macdonalds, Ralston Purina, CocaCola, Schneiders, Prime Restaurants, Cadbury, Apple, Natrel, Lindt, OPG, and the Government of Ontario. He has worked in the USA, England, Holland, South Africa, Australia, Mexico, and New Zealand. Projects in the tourism and hospitality industry include holiday concepts and marketing for clients in Jamaica, Saint Lucia, Barbados, Anguilla, and Cuba.

John's work with Pangaea ensures that he is now eating better than ever. His mum's delighted.

To contact John, email speakmans@roger.com.

Jesse Gibson

Jesse Gibson is a graduate of interactive and graphic design. He started his career at Ranscombe & Co., where he worked with clients such as the Australian Boot Company, Ontario Science Centre, and the National Magazine Award Foundation. He later went on to start a thriving freelance career that included work for the United Way of Toronto. For the past five years Jesse has worked as Design Director at Partners and Edell. His graphic and advertising work includes fully integrated campaigns for the Ontario Ministry of Health, Ontario Power Generation, the Jane Goodall Institute, the Canadian Breast Cancer Foundation, and Kids Help Phone.

To see what Jesse has been up to lately, check out www.jgibson.ca.

James Tse

Photographer James Tse's work focuses on food, people, environment, and still life images. His work has been recognized with numerous awards and he shoots for a variety of editorial and advertising clients in Toronto, New York, and Los Angeles. James has recently completed a selection of innovative cookbook projects.

While working on *Pangaea — Why It Tastes So Good*, James cultivated a deep appreciation for the local and organic food movements that Pangaea has supported for many years. He particularly enjoyed meeting local farmers and food producers who, through ingenuity and hard work, have committed themselves to producing healthy, high-quality food.

For more information or to contact James, visit www.jamestsephoto.com.

Lucie Richard

From billboards to websites, Lucie Richard is the go-to food stylist for advertising, editorial, packaging, and the web designers who recognize her talent. A former chef and associate food editor, Lucie helped to make many of the images in *Pangaea. Why It Tastes So Good.* picture perfect.

Besides being the food stylist Martin turned to for help with this project's more complex photos, Lucie and her chef husband, Jean-Jacques Texier, are Martin's friends and share his appreciation for good food and good wine. While working on this book, Lucie not only practised her craft but also worked side by side with Martin so that he could ensure that the portrayal of every dish matches his aesthetic. Needless to say, Lucie is a woman of incredible patience.

For more information or to contact Lucie, visit www.lucierichard.ca.

Photo Credits

Books have a lot in common with children. For instance, the saying goes that it takes a village to raise a child and, as the photo credit list below illustrates, the same support is necessary to bring a book like this one to a stage of maturity suitable for publication.

While James Tse was the creative force behind most of the picutes in this book, he couldn't be with me 24–7 during the 14 years it took Pangaea to become the restaurant it is today. As a result, we gathered photos from a wide range of sources to round out the excellent images James created during the almost two years we worked together.

Other photo contributors include:

Suresh Doss: page 2–3, page 27 (hostess)
Roman Kliotzkin: page 15
Ronald Francis (personal collection): page 19 (Prince Charles and Martin Kouprie)
Martin Kouprie: pages 26, 28–29, 42–43, 44, 49, 58, 69, 86, 100, 111, 120, 122, 138, 149, 151, 153, 159, 163, 180, 197, 199, 201, 203, 206, 208–209, 214, 222
Chris Freeland: page 118–119
Istock Photo: page 170
Head shots supplied by subjects: page 223

Photo montages on pages 18–19, 30–31, 32–33, 38–39 feature a combination of shots taken by James Tse, Suresh Doss and Martin Kouprie.